MODERN
Crocheted
BLANKETS, THROWS
& CUSHIONS

MODERN *Crocheted*
BLANKETS, THROWS & CUSHIONS

35 colourful, cosy and comfortable patterns

Laura Strutt

CICO BOOKS
LONDON NEW YORK

Dedication

To Ethan Wolf – welcome to the pack Wolfie!

Published in 2018 by CICO Books
an imprint of Ryland Peters & Small Ltd
20–21 Jockey's Fields, London WC1R 4BW

www.rylandpeters.com

10 9 8 7 6 5 4 3 2 1

A CIP catalogue record for this book is available from the British Library.

ISBN: 978 1 78249 638 0

Printed in China

Editor: Marie Clayton
Pattern checker: Jemima Bicknell
Photographer: Emma Mitchell
Stylist: Nel Haynes
Illustrator: Stephen Dew

Art director: Sally Powell
Production manager: Gordana Simakovic
Publishing manager: Penny Craig
Publisher: Cindy Richards

CONTENTS

INTRODUCTION

Crocheted blankets and cushions never seem to go out of style. Maybe it's because we are often nostalgic for these colourful creations, or because there are so many possible variations. Whether you wrap a blanket around yourself on a cold winter evening, drape a throw over your favourite armchair or cuddle up to a handmade cushion, these crocheted creations are a hug that you can keep!

Growing up with grandmothers who both crocheted, I recall a colourful childhood of blankets on their sofas, cosy comforters for us, and even mini blankets for our dolls and teddies. Like me, many are touched by nostalgia when it comes to crocheted blankets, and many of the designs in this book are inspired by the traditional techniques favoured by my grandmothers. However, when the yarns and colours are carefully selected, crocheted blankets can also offer a boho style or even a modern geometric feel, giving them a wide appeal for a variety of personal styles. Many blankets, throws and cushions can be worked with the repetition of just a handful of stitches, making them ideal for novice crocheters looking to branch out. Others feature more complex colour and stitch techniques, which will give those with more experience a bit of a challenge.

Whether you are making something to give as a gift, or to keep and treasure for yourself, I hope that this collection of colourful and creative designs will inspire you, boost your personal passion for crochet and teach you a few new techniques along the way.

Happy crocheting!

Laura

BEFORE YOU BEGIN

Crocheted blankets, throws and cushions are fabulous projects to make, whether you want to update your decor, or to give them as gifts to be treasured.

This book offers a collection of 35 different patterns, which are ideal projects for discovering new techniques and building your crochet skills, whether you're a seasoned crochet fan or a budding novice. You can also choose from larger scale designs that require a considerable time commitment, or opt for a more modular make, which you can work 'on the go' to fit into your personal schedule.

TIPS AND HINTS

• Blankets and throws are often very large makes. Not only does this mean that they are a commitment in time, but they can also be hard work on the wrists. Reduce the pressure and strain on your wrists by holding the weight of the project in your lap as you work. In addition, larger makes can be off-putting due to how time consuming they are perceived to be. You can always work on them in small, more manageable sections, focusing on one colour or strip pattern repeat per session, and enjoy the process!

• Or course, you may like to change the size of these blankets, making them larger or smaller to suit your requirements. For the most part these designs can be customised by increasing or decreasing the initial foundation chain or by working more or fewer rounds or rows. Just be sure to adjust the yarn quantities accordingly before you begin.

• Larger projects also use larger quantities of yarn, and it is always a good idea to make sure that you have enough yarn before you begin. Also, try to ensure that each ball in a bulk order comes from the same dye lot, as although the shade is the same, you will be surprised at just how much variation can occur from one dye lot to the next – and it can often be noticeable on a finished piece.

• You may prefer to work with a selection of yarns already available in your stash. Substituting yarns for those used in the patterns can be done quickly and easily: simply check the yarn details given in the projects and compare them to the yarn you wish to work with. You can always work a swatch to see whether you will need to size up or size down your crochet hook to match the tension guide.

• Some of the projects, such as the Vintage Lace Granny Squares (page 98) and the Purple Patch blanket (page 56) benefit from being blocked once completed. Blocking will bring the piece to the finished measurements and will help to make a real feature of fancy stitches. In projects like Deep Pinks and Blues (page 33) blocking each individual square before seaming will help the blanket to come together more neatly. Blocking can be done by soaking or spritzing with water and pinning out to the set dimensions to dry – you can

buy purpose-made blocking boards or you can use foam mats or even a bed. You can also use the steam from an iron to help block pieces, covering them first with a pressing cloth to protect the fibres. Different yarns respond better to different methods of blocking – using the heat and steam from an iron can damage acrylic or man-made fibres.

• Some of the patterns in this book – such as Waves of Colour (page 62) and A Stitch in Time (page 30) – feature lots of colour changes, leaving lots of yarn ends to weave in. On larger projects like blankets, this can take a long time at the finishing stages, so try and hold the yarn against the work when you change colours, to weave in the ends as you go (see page 125).

YARN

Blankets and throws can be made from any yarn you like – you can work with anything from hand-dyed yarns from indie spinners, mainstream brands, yarns from your existing stash or even repurposed yarns from old handknits! Of course, all different yarns will have different properties and finishes, which will have an impact on the final pieces. You may prefer to select natural fibres for small babies and children, machine-washable yarns for items you expect to have heavy use, and sumptuous blends of silk or alpaca for extra special gifts.

Alongside the composition of the fibre, the weight of the yarn will affect the finished piece too. Lightweight yarns will be much more floaty than the dense fabric created by using chunkier yarns,

A full description of the yarns – brand, style, fibres, length per ball, weight per ball, shade and amount needed – is included in each of the patterns in this book, to make it easy for you to recreate these designs at home. However, you will also find information on the tension for the project. This will not only help you achieve the look and measurements of the pieces by helping you to select the correct crochet hook to match the tension, but is also useful should you want to make a yarn substitution. The closer the yarn is in composition, style and weight to the yarn listed, the closer to the finished piece the make will be.

With larger makes, like blankets, it is often the case that these are worked on for a while then put away in favour of other makes, before being revisited. While this is often a great way to work on large-scale projects, it is wise to store them in a suitable manner. A sealed box or even a zip-lock bag will keep them away from dust and dirt, and also prevent them getting snagged or damaged while you aren't working on them. Storing them with some dried lavender will give your WIP a fresh scent and ward off moths in the process!

You may want to keep a note of the crochet hook used (if not storing it with your project) so that you won't create any variations in tension by returning to work on a project with the incorrect hook.

EQUIPMENT

Crochet hooks: The patterns in this book indicate the size of hook to use with the yarn listed for the project. You can adjust these where necessary to accommodate yarn substitutions, or to adjust your tension. How you hold your hook is a matter of preference – left-handed or right-handed, some like to hold their hook in a pencil-grip, while others prefer to hold it in their fist like a knife. There is no right or wrong way, as long as you are able to move your wrist freely and can comfortably work neat and even stitches. See page 115 in the techniques section for further guidance.

Locking stitch markers: These can be put in position to indicate the start of a round or the position of an increase or decrease, and you can move them on as you start the next round or row.

Tapestry and yarn needles: These are used to secure the ends of the yarn at the start and end of the project and also where changing colours. For heavier weight yarns, try using a split-eye needle or even a small crochet hook to secure in the ends neatly.

Sewing needle and thread: Handy to have for securing buttons or other fastenings to finished makes.

Tape measure: Always useful for checking tension swatches and finished sizes when blocking.

Rust-proof pins: For holding your project in shape while blocking.

SKILL LEVEL

Each project includes a star rating as a skill level guide and you will find the project includes the techniques listed below:

● ◉ ◉ Projects for first-time crocheters using basic stitches with minimal shaping.

● ● ◉ Projects using yarn with basic stitches, repetitive stitch patterns, simple colour changes and simple shaping and finishing.

● ● ● Projects using a variety of techniques, such as basic lace patterns or colour patterns, mid-level shaping and finishing.

ABBREVIATIONS

alt	alternat(e)ing
approx.	approximately
BLO	back loop only
ch	chain
ch sp(s)	chain space(s)
cm	centimetre(s)
cont	continu(e)ing
dc	double crochet
dc2tog	double crochet 2 stitches together
dec	decreas(e)ing
dtr	double treble
FLO	front loop only
foll	follow(s)ing
g	gram(mes)
htr	half treble
in	inch(es)
inc(s)	increase(s)
m	metre(s)
mm	millimetre(s)
oz	ounce(s)
patt	pattern
rep	repeat
RS	right side
sl st	slip stitch
st(s)	stitch(es)
sp	space
tr	treble
tr2tog	treble crochet 2 stitches together
yd(s)	yard(s)
WS	wrong side
yrh	yarn round hook
[]	work section between square brackets number of times stated
*	asterisk indicates beginning of repeated section of pattern

CHAPTER ONE

BRIGHT *and Beautiful*

RAINBOW *Mandala*

This large lap blanket is a colourful take on a traditional granny design. Worked to create a giant circle, the vibrant pattern repeats play up the boho style.

SKILL RATING: ● ● ○

MATERIALS
Stylecraft Special DK (100% acrylic, approx. 295m/322yd per 100g/3½oz ball) DK (light worsted) weight yarn:
1 ball each of shades:
Silver 1203 (A)
Pomegranate 1083 (B)
Spice 1711 (C)
Saffron 1081 (D)
Lime 1712 (E)
Aster 1003 (F)
Magenta 1084 (G)
Violet 1277 (H)
Cream 1005 (I)
4mm (US size G/6) hook
Yarn needle

FINISHED MEASUREMENTS
Finished blanket is 145cm (57in) in diameter

TENSION (GAUGE)
First 3 rounds measure 9cm (3½in) in diameter.

ABBREVIATIONS
See page 9.

For the blanket

Using a 4mm (US size G/6) hook and yarn A, make a magic ring.

Round 1: Ch3 (counts as 1tr throughout), 1tr into the ring, [ch1, 2tr into the ring] 5 times, ch1, join with a sl st in 3rd of 3-ch. *Six 2-tr groups.*

Round 2: Sl st in next st, join in yarn B, sl st in ch sp, ch3, (1tr, ch1, 2tr) in same sp, *ch1, (2tr, ch1, 2tr) in next ch sp; rep from * to end of round, ch1, join with a sl st in 3rd of 3-ch. *Twelve 2-tr groups.*

Round 3: Sl st in next st, join in yarn C, sl st in ch sp, ch4 (counts as 1tr and ch1 throughout), 3tr in next ch sp, *ch1, 3tr in next ch sp; rep from * to end of round, ch1, 2tr in same ch sp as first sl st, join with a sl st in 3rd of 4-ch. *Twelve 3-tr groups.*

Round 4: Join in yarn D, sl st in ch sp, ch3, 2tr in same sp, *ch1, 3tr in next ch sp; rep from * to end of round, ch1, join with a sl st in 3rd of 3-ch.

Round 5 (inc): Join in yarn E, ch4, *(3tr, ch1, 3tr) in next ch sp, ch1; rep from * to last ch sp, (3tr, ch1, 2tr) in last ch sp, join with a sl st in 3rd of 4-ch. *Twenty-four 3-tr groups.*

Round 6: Join in yarn F, sl st in ch sp, ch3, 2tr in same sp, *ch1, 3tr in next ch sp; rep from * to end of round, ch1, join with a sl st in 3rd of 3-ch.

Round 7: Join in yarn G, ch4, 3tr in next ch sp, *ch1, 3tr in next ch sp; rep from * to last ch sp, 2tr in last ch sp, join with a sl st in 3rd of 4-ch.

Round 8: Join in yarn H, sl st in ch sp, ch3, 2tr in same sp, *ch1, 3tr in next ch sp; rep from * to end of round, ch1, join with a sl st in 3rd of 3-ch.

MAKE IT YOURS / This blanket is made with a rainbow-striped design; alternatively you can work in colour blocks, but be sure to adjust yarn amounts accordingly.

The increases are worked every 5th round, and 12 groups will be added on each increase round. Keep track of the row count so as to not lose your place in the pattern.

Round 9: Join in yarn I, ch4, 3tr in next ch sp, *ch1, 3tr in next ch sp; rep from * to last ch sp, 2tr in last ch sp, join with a sl st in 3rd of 4-ch.

Round 10 (inc): Change to yarn A, sl st in ch sp, ch3, 2tr in same sp, *ch1, (3tr, ch1, 3tr) in next ch sp, ch1, 3tr in next sp; rep from * to last ch sp, ch1 (3tr, ch1, 3tr) in last ch sp, ch1, join with a sl st in 3rd of 3-ch. *Thirty-six 3-tr groups*.

Round 11: Change to yarn B, ch4, 3tr in next ch sp, *ch1, 3tr in next ch sp; rep from * to last ch sp, 2tr in last ch sp, join with a sl st in 3rd of 4-ch.

Round 12: Change to yarn C, sl st in ch sp, ch3, 2tr in same sp, *ch1, 3tr in next ch sp; rep from * to end of round, ch1, join with a sl st in 3rd of 3-ch.

Cont in patt as set, rep colour block patt of yarns A to I until 6 full colour reps have been worked in total and **at the same time** working inc round every 5th round [working one more 3tr group between (3tr, ch1, 3tr) increases on every inc round]. *One hundred and thirty-two 3-tr groups*.

Change to yarn A, work one more inc round as set. *One hundred and forty-four 3-tr groups*.

Change to yarn I, work 2 rounds in patt as set.

FOR THE BORDER

Round 1: Using a 4mm (US size G/6) hook and yarn A, 1dc in each tr and ch sp to end, join with a sl st in first dc. *576 dc*.

Round 2: 1ch (does not count as st), 1dc in each dc to end, join with a sl st in first dc.

Fasten off.

Making up and finishing

Weave in all ends and block as desired to neaten.

CANDYFLOSS *Colours*

This striking pattern is created with the simple repetition of two rows of stitches – alternating between three colours gives it a bold, modern finish.

MATERIALS

Lion Brand Pound of Love (100% acrylic, approx. 932m/1019yd per 454g/16oz ball) Aran (worsted) weight yarn:
 1 ball each of shades:
  Pastel Blue 106 (A)
  White 100 (B)
  Pink 103 (C)

6mm (US size J/10) hook

Locking stitch markers/safety pins (optional)

Yarn needle

FINISHED MEASUREMENTS

Finished blanket is 96.5 x157.5cm (38 x 62in)

TENSION (GAUGE)

Five 3-tr groups x 10 rows = 10cm (4in) square, using a 6mm (US size J/10) hook.

ABBREVIATIONS

See page 9.

For the blanket

Using a 6mm (US size J/10) hook and yarn A, work a foundation ch of 151 sts.

Row 1: 1dc in 3rd ch from hook (missed 2-ch does not count as st or 2-ch sp), *ch2, miss 2 ch, 1dc in next ch; rep from * to last 4 ch, ch2, miss 2 ch, 1dc in each of next 2 ch, turn. *51 sts + forty-nine 2-ch sps.*

Row 2: Ch3 (counts as 1tr), 3tr in first ch-2 sp made in previous row, *3tr in next ch-2 sp made in previous row; rep from * to end, 1tr in last dc, turn. *149 sts.*

Row 3: Join in yarn B, ch1, 1dc in sp between 1-tr and 3-tr made in previous row, *ch2, 1dc between next 2 sets of 3-tr; rep from * to end, ch2, 1dc in 3rd of 3-ch, turn. *50 sts + forty-nine 2-ch sps.*
Rows 2 and 3 form Block Stitch patt. Rep these 2 rows, alt between yarn C and yarn A for row 2 and always using yarn B for row 3, until work measures 155cm (61in), ending with row 2 worked in yarn A.
Cont with yarn A, work row 3. Do not turn.

Tips

The foundation chain is very long; to help keep count, add locking stitch markers every 25 chain stitches.

Weave in the ends as much as possible as you go, then you can secure the tails when working the border round the outer edge.

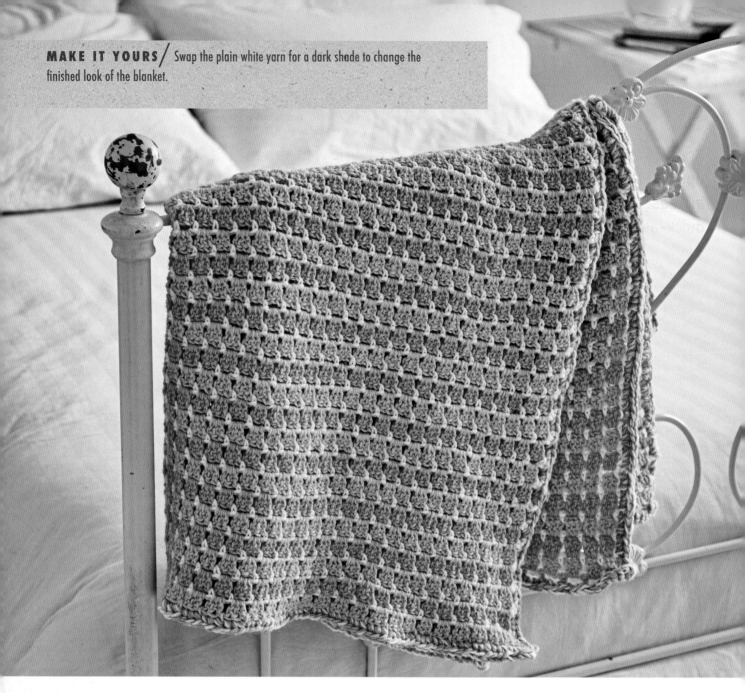

FOR THE BORDER

Using a 6mm (US size J/10) hook and holding yarns A, B and C as one, work 3dc in each tr sp along first side, (1dc, ch1, 1dc) in first corner, 3dc in each ch sp along bottom, (1dc, ch1, 1dc) in 2nd corner, 3dc in each tr sp along 2nd side, (1dc, ch1, 1dc) in 3rd corner, 3dc in each ch sp along top, (1dc, ch1, 1dc) in 4th corner, join with a sl st in first dc.
Fasten off.

Making up and finishing

Weave in all ends and block as desired to neaten.

SUNNY *Skies*

Create a geometric design with ultra-modern fabric yarn, for an instant update to your interiors. This classic hexagon is formed by adding simple increases while working in the round. Made in a super-thick yarn, this is a quick-and-easy make for beginners and more experienced crocheters alike.

SKILL RATING: ● ○ ○

MATERIALS
Lion Brand Fast-Track (60% cotton, 40% polyester, approx. 136m/149yd per 227g/8oz ball) super chunky (super bulky) weight yarn:
  3 balls of shade Chopper Grey 149 (A)
  2 balls of shade Taxi Cab Yellow 157 (B)
  3 balls of shade Cruise Ship Aqua 102 (C)

15mm (US size Q) hook

Locking stitch marker or safety pin

Yarn needle or smaller crochet hook

FINISHED MEASUREMENTS
Finished blanket measures 112cm (44in) along each straight side

TENSION (GAUGE)
Exact tension is not essential for this project.

ABBREVIATIONS
See page 9.

For the hexagon

Using a 15mm (US size Q) hook and yarn A, make a magic ring.
Round 1: Ch3 (counts as 1tr), 1tr into the ring, *ch1, 2tr into the ring; rep from * 4 more times, ch1, join with a sl st in 3rd of 3-ch. *12 tr + six 1-ch sps.*
Round 2: Ch4 (counts as 1tr and ch1), *(2tr, ch2, 2tr) in next 1-ch sp, ch1; rep from * 4 more times, (2tr, ch2, 1tr) in last 1-ch sp, join with a sl st in 3rd of 3-ch. *24 tr + six 2-ch sps + six 1-ch sps.*

This blanket is worked in the round from a central magic ring; you can place a locking stitch marker at the start of every round to help you keep on track.

Round 3: Sl st in first ch sp, ch3 (counts as 1tr), 1tr in same ch sp, ch1, *(2tr, ch2, 2tr) in next 2-ch sp, ch1, 2tr in next 1-ch sp, ch1; rep from * 4 more times, (2tr, ch2, 2tr) in next 2-ch sp, ch1, join with a sl st in 3rd of 3-ch. *36 tr + six 2-ch sps + twelve 1-ch sps.*
Cont in patt as set, using foll colour sequence:
  Yarn A for 1 round.
  Yarn B for 2 rounds.
  Yarn C for 2 rounds.
  Yarn A for 2 rounds
  Yarn B for 2 rounds.
  Yarn C for 2 rounds
  Yarn A for 2 rounds.
  Yarn B for 2 rounds.
  Yarn C for 2 rounds.

FOR THE BORDER
Change to yarn A.
Next round: Ch1, 1dc in each st and 1-ch sp, and 2dc in each 2-ch sp, to end of round, join with a sl st in first dc. *366 dc.*
Next round: Ch1, 1dc in each st to end, join with a sl st in first dc.
Fasten off.

Making up and finishing

Weave in all ends and block as desired to neaten.

Chunky yarn like this doesn't always fit through the eye of a yarn needle. You can always use a small crochet hook instead to help you weave the ends in neatly.

MAKE IT YOURS / For a denser, thicker make – or to create a rug – double the yarn quantities and hold two strands of yarn together throughout.

MAKE IT YOURS / This throw can be increased in size, just ensure that the number of stitches in the foundation chain is a multiple of 29 plus 3.

SALTWATER *Toffee*

A chevron is a geometric motif that simply never goes out of style.
This soft bedrunner in seaside colours is worked in double crochet, with
texture added by working into the back loops, giving it a distinctive finish.

SKILL RATING: ● ● ○

MATERIALS

Caron Simply Soft (100% acrylic,
approx. 288m/314yd per 170g/6oz ball)
Aran (worsted) weight yarn:
   3 balls of shade White 9701 (A)
   2 balls each of shades:
      Sage 9705 (B)
      Autumn Maize 0008 (C)
      Strawberry 0015 (D)

5.5mm (US size I/9) hook

Yarn needle

FINISHED MEASUREMENTS

Finished blanket is 117 x 157.5cm
(46 x 62in)

TENSION (GAUGE)

Exact tension is not essential for this
project.

ABBREVIATIONS

See page 9.

For the throw

Using a 5.5mm (US size I/9) hook and yarn A, work a foundation ch of
177 sts.
Row 1: Beg in 2nd ch from hook, *dc2tog, 1dc in each of next 13 ch,
3dc in next ch, 1dc in each of next 13 ch, rep from * to last 2 ch,
dc2tog, turn. *181 sts.*
Note: Work in BLO of all dc sts.
Row 2: Ch1 (does not count as st throughout), dc2tog, 1dc in each
of next 13 dc, 3dc in next dc, *1dc in each of next 13 dc, miss next
2 dc, 1dc in each of next 14 dc, 3dc in next dc; rep from * to last
15 dc, 1dc in each of next 13 dc, dc2tog. *181 sts.*

Row 2 forms patt, cont in patt as set using foll colour sequence:
   Yarn B for 4 rows.
   Yarn A for 2 rows.
   Yarn C for 4 rows.
   Yarn A for 2 rows.
   Yarn D for 4 rows.
   Yarn A for 2 rows.

Rep this colour block 7 more times (8 times in total) until work
measures 157.5cm (62in), ending after 2 rows in yarn A.
Fasten off.

Making up and finishing

Weave in all ends and block as desired to neaten.

Make sure that you work through the back
loops only of the double crochet stitches,
as this is what gives the blanket its unique
textured finish.

Changing yarn colour every few rows leaves
lots of loose ends to weave in; hold the ends
of the yarn against the work as you change
colour and work the stitches to secure the
ends as you go. You might also like to carry
the white yarn up the sides to save cutting it
at each change.

Sunburst Squares
BLANKET

This bright and colourful granny square motif is a firm favourite and it is one that will never go out of style. These classic squares are joined-as-you-go, so you will be surprised how quickly this blanket can be made!

SKILL RATING: ● ● ○

MATERIALS
Paintbox Yarns Simply Aran (100% acrylic, approx. 184m/201yd per 100g/3½oz ball) DK (light worsted) weight yarn:
  9 balls of shade Champagne White 202 (A)
  1 ball each of shades:
    Slate Grey 205 (B)
    Melon Sorbet 216 (C)
    Pansy Purple 247 (D)
    Mustard Yellow 223 (E)
    Vintage Pink 255 (F)
    Slate Green 226 (G)
    Raspberry Pink 243 (H)
    Dolphin Blue 236 (I)
    Pale Lilac 245 (J)
    Misty Grey 203 (K)
5.5mm (US size I/9) and 6mm (US size J/10) hooks
Yarn needle

FINISHED MEASUREMENTS
Finished blanket is 132 x 162cm (52 x 64in)

TENSION (GAUGE)
Each square measures 15cm (6in) square, using 5.5mm (US size I/9) hook.

ABBREVIATIONS
See page 9.

SPECIAL ABBREVIATIONS
PS (puff stitch) – *yrh, insert hook in st, yrh, draw yarn through; rep from * 3 more times (7 loops on hook), yrh, draw through all 7 loops, ch1 to close st
3trcl (3-treble cluster) – *yrh, insert hook in ch sp, yrh, draw yarn through, yrh draw yarn through first 2 loops; rep from * twice more (4 loops on hook), yrh, draw through all 4 loops
4trcl (4-treble cluster) – *yrh, insert hook in ch sp, yrh, draw yarn through, yrh draw yarn through first 2 loops; rep from * 3 more times (5 loops on hook), yrh, draw through all 5 loops

For the blanket

STARBURST GRANNY SQUARE

Using a 5.5mm (US size I/9) hook and yarn B, make a magic ring.
Round 1: Ch3 (counts as 1tr), 15tr into ring, join with a sl st in 3rd of 3-ch. *16 sts*.
Round 2: Join yarn C (or 2nd colour), ch1, PS in first tr, ch1, *(PS in next tr), ch1; rep from * to end, join with a sl st in first PS. *16 PS*.
Fasten off 2nd colour.
Round 3: Join yarn D (or 3rd colour) in first ch sp, ch2, 3trcl (counts as 4trcl) in same sp, ch1, *4trcl in next ch sp, ch1; rep from * to end, join with a sl st in top of 3trcl.
Fasten off 3rd colour.
Round 4: Join yarn A in first ch sp, ch2 (counts as 1htr), 2htr in same sp, 3htr in each of next 2 ch sps, (3tr, ch2, 3tr) in next ch sp for corner, *3htr in each of next 3 ch sps, (3tr, ch2, 3tr) in next ch-sp for corner; rep from * twice more, join with a sl st in 2nd of 2-ch.
Round 5: Sl st in each of first 2 sts, sl st in sp between clusters, ch3 (counts as 1tr), 2tr in same sp, ch1, [3tr in next sp between clusters, ch1] twice, *(3tr, ch3, 3tr) in next 2-ch sp for corner, ch1, [3tr in next sp between clusters, ch1] 4 times; rep from * twice more, (3tr, ch3, 3tr) in last 2-ch sp for corner, ch1, 3tr in next sp between clusters, ch1 join with a sl st in 3rd of 3-ch.
Fasten off.
Make 80 squares in total, using a combination of colours for each round, mix and match as you go for a more eclectic style. Round 1 is always worked in yarn B and rounds 4 and 5 are worked in yarn A. Join-as-you-go as follows:

JOIN-AS-YOU-GO

Once one square is complete the square next to it can be joined on in the final round. This is done at each corner 3-ch sp and every 1-ch sp along sides of each joining edge or edges by passing the loop of the stitch that you are making on the current square through the corresponding stitches of the other square, before continuing with the stitch. Continue in this manner adding on each new square as the round is worked. Make 10 rows of 8 blocks.

FOR THE BORDER

Round 1: With RS facing, using a 6mm (US size J/10) hook, join yarn K in first 1-ch sp after any corner, ch3 (counts as 1tr), 2tr in same sp, *3tr in each ch-sp to next corner, (3tr, ch1, 3tr) in corner sp; rep from * 3 more times, join with a sl st in 3rd of 3-ch.
Round 2: Sl st in each of next 2 sts, sl st in sp between clusters, ch3 (counts as 1tr), 2tr in same sp, *3tr in each sp between clusters to next corner, (3tr, ch1, 3tr) in corner sp; rep from * 3 more times, 3tr in next sp between clusters, join with a sl st in 3rd of 3-ch.
Round 3: Change to yarn A, ch1, *1dc in each st to next corner, (1dc, ch1, 1dc) in corner sp; rep from * 3 more times, 1dc in each st to end, join with a sl st in first dc.
Fasten off.

Making up and finishing

Weave in all ends and block as desired to neaten.

DIAMOND *Brights*

This variation of the classic granny square uses the combination of half trebles, trebles and double trebles to makes stitches of varying heights.

SKILL RATING: ● ● ●

MATERIALS

Stylecraft Special DK (100% acrylic, approx. 295m/322yd per 100g/3½oz ball) DK (light worsted) weight yarn:
1 ball each of shades:
Aster 1003 (A)
Cloud Blue 1019 (B)
Sherbet 1034 (C)
Empire 1829 (D)
Saffron 1081 (E)
Turquoise 1068 (F)
Violet 1277 (G)
Aspen 1422 (H)
Pistachio 1822 (I)
Sunshine 1114 (J)
Fuchsia Purple 1827 (K)
Lime 1712 (L)
Spice 1711 (M)
Tomato 1723 N)
Magenta 1084 (O)
Pomegranate 1083 (P)
Cream 1005 (Q)

4mm (US size G/6) hook

Yarn needle

FINISHED MEASUREMENTS

Finished blanket is 86 x 127cm (34 x 50in).

TENSION (GAUGE)

Each square measures 19cm (7½in) diagonally at widest point, using 4mm (US size G/6) hook.

ABBREVIATIONS

See page 9.

For the blanket

DIAMOND BLOCK (MAKE 3 IN EACH COLOUR, 48 IN TOTAL)

Using a 4mm (US size G/6) hook and yarn A, make a magic ring.

Round 1: Ch3 (counts as 1tr throughout), 2tr into the ring, *ch2, 3tr into the ring; rep from * twice more, ch2, join with a sl st in 3rd of 3-ch.

Round 2: Ch5 (counts as 1dtr and ch1), (3htr, ch2, 3htr) in next 2-ch sp, ch1, (3dtr, ch2, 3dtr) in next 2-ch sp, ch1, (3htr, ch2, 3htr) in next 2-ch sp, ch1, (3dtr, ch2, 2dtr) in last 2-ch sp, join with a sl st in 4th of 5-ch.

Round 3: Ch3, 2tr in first 1-ch sp, ch1, (3htr, ch2, 3htr) in next 2-ch sp, ch1, 3tr in next 1-ch sp, ch1, (3dtr, ch2, 3dtr) in next 2-ch sp, ch1, 3tr in next 1-ch sp, ch1, (3htr, ch2, 3htr) in next 2-ch sp, ch1, 3tr in next 1-ch sp, ch1, (3dtr, ch2, 3dtr) in next 2-ch sp, ch1, join with a sl st in 3rd of 3-ch.

Tips Blocking these diamonds before seaming them together will bring out the shaping.

The centre of the blocks is made with a magic ring; be sure to draw it up fully to neatly close the hole at the centre.

Round 4: Ch4 (counts as 1tr and ch1), 3tr in next 1-ch sp, ch1, (3htr, ch2, 3htr) in next 2-ch sp, ch1, (3tr, ch1) in each of next two 1-ch sps, (3dtr, ch2, 3dtr) in next 2-ch sp, ch1, (3tr, ch1) in each of next two 1-ch sps, (3htr, ch2, 3htr) in next 2-ch sp, ch1, (3tr, ch1) in each of next 2 1-ch sps, (3dtr, ch2, 3dtr) in next 2-ch sp, ch1, 2tr in last 1-ch sp, join with a sl st in 3rd of 4-ch.

Round 5: Ch3, 2tr in first 1-ch sp, ch1, 3tr in next 1-ch sp, ch1, (3htr, ch2, 3htr) in next 2-ch sp, ch1, (3tr, ch1) in each of next three 1-ch sps, (3dtr, ch2, 3dtr) in next 2-ch sp, ch1, (3tr, ch1) in each of next three 1-ch sps, (3htr, ch2, 3htr) in next 2-ch sp, ch1, (3tr, ch1) in each of next three 1-ch sps, (3dtr, ch2, 3dtr) in next 2-ch sp, ch1, 3tr in last 1-ch sp, ch1, join with a sl st in 3rd of 3-ch. Fasten off.

Making up and finishing

Place all diamond blocks into desired pattern in eight rows of six.

Using a 4mm (US size G/6) hook and yarn Q, join the blocks together with 1dc in each stitch, working through both layers. Work around each block to join it to the surrounding shapes, this will create a finished border once all the seaming is complete.

Weave in all ends and block as desired to neaten.

MAKE IT YOURS / Create a repeating pattern by positioning the diamond blocks in your chosen design before seaming up.

A STITCH IN *Time*

This large lap blanket features a host of bright yarns and range of stitches to create a sampler effect. It is ideal for working with yarns from your stash.

SKILL RATING: ● ● ●

MATERIALS

Cascade 220 (100% Peruvian highland wool, approx. 200m/220yd per 100g/3½oz ball) Aran (worsted) weight yarn:
  4 balls of shade Grey 8509 (A)
  1 ball each of shades:
    Blue Hawaii 9421 (B)
    Bright Red 8414 (C)
    Mineral Blue 8311 (D)
    Butter 8687 (E)
    Deep Lavender 8762 (F)
    Azalea 9610 (G)
    Nectarine 2451 (H)

6mm (US size J/10) hook

Yarn needle

FINISHED MEASUREMENTS

Finished blanket is 112 x 122cm (44 x 48in)

TENSION (GAUGE)

12 tr x 6 rows = 10cm (4in) square in tr, using 6mm (US size J/10) hook.

ABBREVIATIONS

See page 9.

SPECIAL ABBREVIATION

3trcl (3-treble cluster) – *yrh, insert hook in ch sp, yrh, draw yarn through, yrh, draw yarn through first 2 loops; rep from * twice more (4 loops on hook), yrh, draw through all 4 loops

For the blanket

Using a 6mm (US size J/10) hook and yarn A, work a foundation ch of 127 sts.

Row 1: 1tr in 3rd ch from hook (missed 2-ch doesn't count as st), 1tr in each st to end. *125 tr.*

Row 2: Ch3 (counts as 1tr throughout), 1tr in each st to end.

Rep row 2 thirty-four more times, 36 rows in total.

Row 37: Change to yarn B, ch1 (does not count as st throughout), 1dc in each tr to end. *125 dc.*

Row 38: Change to yarn A, ch1, 1dc in each dc to end.

Rows 39–41: Using yarn C, ch3, 1tr in each st to end. *125 tr.*

Row 42: Change to yarn D, ch3, miss first 2 sts, 3tr in next st, *miss next 2 sts, 3tr in next st; rep from * to last 2 sts, miss 1 st, 1tr in last st.

Rows 43–44: Using yarn E, ch3, 1tr in each st to end. *125 tr.*

Row 45: Change to yarn F, ch1, 1dc in each st to end. *125 dc.*

Row 46: Ch4 (counts as 1tr and ch1 throughout), miss first 2 sts, *1tr in next st, ch2, miss next 2 sts; rep from * to last 3 sts, 1tr in next st, ch1, miss 1 st, 1tr in last st.

Row 47: Change to yarn C, ch3, 1tr in next ch sp, 1tr in next st, *2tr in next ch sp, 1 tr in next st; rep from * to last ch sp, 1tr in ch sp, 1tr in last st. *125 tr.*

Tip

If using yarns from your stash, be sure to pick ones of the same weight, so that the tension remains the same throughout.

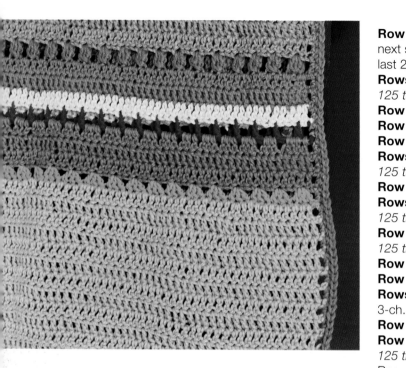

Row 48: Change to yarn G, ch4, miss first 2 sts, 3trcl in next st, *ch2, miss next 2 sts, 3trcl in next st; rep from * to last 2 sts, miss 1 st, ch1, 1tr in last st.

Rows 49–51: Using yarn D, ch3, 1tr in each st to end. *125 tr.*

Row 52: Change to yarn B, rep row 46.

Row 53: Using yarn B, rep row 47.

Row 54: Change to yarn E, rep row 42.

Rows 55–57: Using yarn H, ch3, 1tr in each st to end. *125 tr.*

Row 58: Change to yarn F, rep row 48.

Rows 59–60: Using yarn G, ch3, 1tr in each st to end. *125 tr.*

Row 61: Change to yarn E, ch3, 1tr in each st to end. *125 tr.*

Row 62: Change to C, rep row 46.

Row 63: Change to yarn F, rep row 47. *125 tr.*

Rows 64–65: Ch3, 1tr in each st to end, 1tr in 3rd of 3-ch.

Row 66: Change to yarn B, rep row 42.

Row 67: Change to yarn A, ch3, 1tr in each st to end. *125 tr.*

Rep row 67 eleven more times.

Fasten off.

FOR THE BORDER

Round 1: With RS facing, using 6mm (US size J/10) hook, join yarn F in first st after top right corner, ch1, *1dc in each st to next corner, (1dc, ch1, 1dc) in corner, 2dc in each row end to next corner, (1dc, ch1, 1dc) in corner; rep from * once more, join with a sl st in first dc.

Round 2: Ch1, *1dc in each st to next corner, (1dc, ch1, 1dc) in corner sp; rep from * 3 more times, 1dc in each st to end, join with a sl st in first dc.

Fasten off.

Making up and finishing

Weave in all ends and block as desired to neaten.

MAKE IT YOURS / Why not use up more scraps from your stash and make a multi-coloured fringe or tassels?

DEEP *Pinks and Blues*

Give this simple motif a fresh look with bright, bold shades. This modular design is made up of lots of squares seamed together, making it a fun and portable project.

SKILL RATING: ● ● ○

MATERIALS

Rowan Summerlite DK (100% cotton, approx. 130m/142yd per 50g/1¾oz ball) DK (light worsted) weight yarn:
  3 balls each of shades:
    Fuchsia 455 (A)
    Indigo 450 (D)
    Lagoon 457 (E)
  2 balls each of shades:
    Rouge 462 (B)
    Summer 453 (C)

4mm (US size G/6) hook

Yarn needle

FINISHED MEASUREMENTS

Finished blanket is 88 x 104cm (35 x 41in)

TENSION (GAUGE)

16 tr x 8 rows = 10cm (4in) square in tr, using 4mm (US size G/6) hook.

Each square measures 12.5cm (5in), using 4mm (US size G/6) hook.

ABBREVIATIONS

See page 9.

For the blanket

SOLID GRANNY SQUARE (MAKE 42)

Using a 4mm (US size G/6) hook and yarn A, make a magic ring.
Round 1: Ch3 (counts as 1tr throughout), 2tr into the ring, *(ch2, 3tr) into the ring; rep from * twice more, ch2, join with a sl st in 3rd of 3-ch.
Round 2: Change to yarn B, ch3, 1tr in each of next 2 sts, (2tr, 2ch, 2tr) in ch sp, *1tr in each of next 3 sts, (2tr, 2ch, 2tr) in ch sp; rep from * twice more, join with a sl st in 3rd of 3-ch.

Tip You may find that blocking each individual square before you seam them together makes the blanket much neater.

Round 3: Change to yarn C, ch3, 1tr in each of next 4 sts, (2tr, 2ch, 2tr) in ch sp, *1tr in each of next 7 sts, (2tr, 2ch, 2tr) in ch sp; rep from * twice more, 1tr in each of next 2 sts, join with a sl st in 3rd of 3-ch.

Round 4: Change to yarn D, ch3, 1tr in each of next 6 sts, (2tr, 2ch, 2tr) in ch sp, *1tr in each of next 11 sts, (2tr, 2ch, 2tr) in ch sp; rep from * twice more, 1tr in each of next 4 sts, join with a sl st in 3rd of 3-ch.

Round 5: Change to yarn E, ch3, 1tr in each of next 8 sts, (2tr, 2ch, 2tr) in ch sp, *1tr in each of next 15 sts, (2tr, 2ch, 2tr) in ch sp; rep from * twice more, 1tr in each of next 6 sts, join with a sl st in 3rd of 3-ch.
Fasten off.

Making up and finishing

Arrange the blocks into seven rows of six. Using a 4mm (US size G/6) crochet hook and yarn A, join the blocks together with 1dc in each st through both layers, working through BLO.

FOR THE BORDER

Rounds 1–3: With RS facing, using a 4mm (US size G/6) hook, join yarn A in first st after any corner, ch3, *1tr in each st to next corner, (2tr, ch2, 2tr) in corner; rep from * 3 more times, join with a sl st in first 3rd of 3-ch.
Fasten off.
Weave in all ends and block as desired to neaten.

MAKE IT YOURS / Alternate the colour sequence of each block for a more unique finish.

Picnic TIME

Create a classic chequerboard design by working in blocks of colour across the row – this blanket carries the yarn across the work so there aren't as many ends to weave in as you might expect!

SKILL RATING: ● ● ●

MATERIALS
Caron One Pound (100% acrylic, approx. 742m/811yd per 454g/16oz ball) Aran (worsted) weight yarn:
  1 ball each of shades:
    White 10501 (A)
    Sky Blue 10508 (B)
    Pale Royal Blue 10624 (C)
6mm (US size J/10) hook
Yarn needle

FINISHED MEASUREMENTS
Finished blanket is 114cm (45in) square

TENSION (GAUGE)
10 tr x 5 rows = 10cm (4in), using 6mm (US size J/10) hook.

ABBREVIATIONS
See page 9.

For the blanket

Using a 6mm (US size J/10) hook and yarn A, work a foundation ch of 112 sts.
Row 1: 1tr in 3rd ch from hook (missed 2-ch doesn't count as st), 1tr in each of next 9 sts, *change to yarn B (carrying yarn A), 1tr in each of next 10 sts, change to yarn A (carrying yarn B), 1tr in each of next 10 sts; rep from * to end. *11 colour blocks ending with yarn A.*
Rows 2–6: Beg with yarn A, ch3 (counts as 1tr throughout), 1tr in each of next 9 sts, *change to yarn B (carrying yarn A), 1tr in each of next 10 sts, change to yarn A (carrying yarn B), 1tr in each of next 10 sts; rep from * to end.

When changing colours on each block, introduce the new colour by taking it through to complete the last part of the final treble worked in the previous colour.

Try to maintain an even tension when carrying the non-working yarn so as not to draw up the stitches.

Rows 7–12: Beg with yarn B, ch3, 1tr in each of next 9 sts, *change to yarn C (carrying yarn B), 1tr in each of next 10 sts, change to yarn B (carrying yarn C), 1tr in each of next 10 sts; rep from * to end.
Rep rows 1 to 12 four more times.
Rep rows 1 to 6 once more, to create 11 blocks of colour by 11 rows of colour blocks.

FOR THE BORDER

Rounds 1–2: With RS facing, using a 6mm (US size J/10) hook, join yarn C in first st after any corner, ch1, *1dc in each st to next corner, (1dc, ch1, 1dc) in corner; rep from * 3 more times, join with a sl st in first dc.
Round 3: Change to yarn A, ch1, *1dc in each st to next corner, (1dc, ch1, 1dc) in corner; rep from * 3 more times, join with a sl st in first dc.
Round 4: Change to yarn C in first st after any corner, ch1, *1dc in each st to next corner, (1dc, ch1, 1dc) in corner; rep from * 3 more times, join with a sl st in first dc. Fasten off.

Making up and finishing

Weave in all ends and block as desired to neaten.

MAKE IT YOURS/ Create this blanket in your preferred colourway by selecting two shades – a light and dark – of the same colour and team with white.

CORNER-TO-CORNER *Colour*

Play up the diagonal design of this cushion, which is worked from one corner to the opposite corner, by using bold blocks of colour.

MATERIALS

Bernat Satin (100% acrylic, approx. 182m/200yd per 100g/3½oz ball) Aran (worsted) weight yarn:
  2 balls of shade Camel 04010 (A)
  1 ball each of shades:
    Maitai 04732 (B)
    Fern 04222 (C)
    Lavender 04309 (D)

5mm (US size H/8) hook

Yarn needle

63cm (25in) square cushion pad

Cushion cover or fabric to create backing

FINISHED MEASUREMENTS

Finished cushion is 63cm (25in) square

TENSION (GAUGE)

Five 3-tr blocks x 5 rows = 10cm (4in) square in stitch patt, using 5mm (US size H/8) hook.

ABBREVIATIONS

See page 9.

For the cushion

Using a 5mm (US size H/8) hook and yarn A, work a foundation ch of 6 sts.

Row 1: 1tr in 4th ch from hook, 1tr in each of next 2 sts. *One 3-tr block.*

Row 2: Turn work, ch6, 1tr in 4th ch from hook, 1tr in each of next 2 sts, sl st in ch sp on block from previous row, ch3 (counts as 1tr), 3tr in same sp. *Two 3-tr blocks.*

Row 3: Turn work, ch6, 1tr in 4th ch from hook, 1tr in each of next 2 sts, sl st in ch sp on first block from previous row, ch3 (counts as 1tr), 3tr in same sp, sl st in ch sp on 2nd block from previous row, ch3 (counts as 1tr), 3tr in same sp. *Three 3-tr blocks.*

Cont in patt as set for a further 4 rows, 7 rows in total. *Seven 3-tr blocks.*

Cont in patt as set, working foll colour sequence:

Yarn B for 4 rows. *Eleven 3-tr blocks.*
Yarn C for 8 rows. *Nineteen 3-tr blocks.*
Yarn D for 4 rows. *Twenty-three 3-tr blocks.*
Yarn A for 6 rows. *Twenty-nine 3-tr blocks.*

BEGIN DECREASING

Cont with yarn A, turn work, sl st in 3 sts on first block in row, *sl st in ch sp on next block from previous row, ch3 (counts as 1tr), 3tr in same sp; rep from * to last block, sl st in ch sp on last block, turn for next row.
This sets patt for dec, cont in dec patt as set in foll colour sequence until one block remains:
Yarn A for 20 rows. *Eight 3-tr blocks*.
Yarn B for 7 rows. *One 3-tr block*.
Fasten off.

Making up and finishing

Weave in all ends and block as desired to neaten.
Place panel onto front of fabric cushion cover and stitch to secure.

To create your own fabric backing, cut two pieces of fabric to 45 x 67.5cm (18 x 27in). Fold 2.5cm (1in) to the WS around each side, press and sew in place. Place the two pieces together, both with RS facing up, to create a 62.5cm (25in) square panel – the pieces will overlap in the centre to allow the cushion pad to be inserted. With WS together, place the assembled fabric piece onto the crochet panel and sew around the outer edges.

MAKE IT YOURS / Make a double-sided cushion by doubling the yarn amounts and making two panels, then join to make a cushion front and back.

NEON *Lights*

This striking home decor make is created by wrapping an oversized granny square around a cushion pad – it's great as a floor cushion, too.

SKILL RATING: ● ● ●

MATERIALS
Rowan Handknit Cotton DK (100% cotton, approx. 85m/93yd per 50g/1¾oz ball) DK (light worsted) weight yarn:
  2 balls each of shades:
    Flamingo 368 (A)
    Gooseberry 219 (C)
    Bleached 263 (D)
  5 balls of shade Slate 347 (B)

4.5mm (US size 7) hook

66cm (26in) square cushion pad

Yarn needle

FINISHED MEASUREMENTS
Finished cushion is 66cm (26in) square

TENSION (GAUGE)
First 3 rounds measure 9cm (3½in) square.

ABBREVIATIONS
See page 9.

For the cushion

Using a 4.5mm (US size 7) hook and yarn A, make a magic ring.
Round 1: Ch3 (counts as 1tr), 2tr into the ring, *ch2, 3tr into the ring; rep from * twice more, ch2, join with a sl st in 3rd of 3-ch.
Round 2: Ch4 (counts as 1tr and ch1), *(3tr, ch2, 3tr) in next 2-ch sp, ch1; rep from * twice more, (3tr, ch2, 2tr) in last 2-ch sp, join with a sl st in 3rd of 4-ch.
Round 3: Ch3 (counts as 1tr), 2tr in first 1-ch sp, *ch1, (3tr, ch2, 3tr) in next 2-ch sp, ch1, 3tr in next 1-ch sp; rep from * twice more, ch1, (3tr, ch2, 3tr) in last 2-ch sp, ch1, join with a sl st in 3rd of 3-ch.
Round 4: Join in yarn B, ch4 (counts as 1tr and ch1), 3tr in next 1-ch sp, *ch1, (3tr, ch2, 3tr) in next 2-ch sp, ch1, 3tr in next 1-ch sp, ch1, 3tr in next 1-ch sp; rep from * twice more, ch1, (3tr, ch2, 3tr) in next 2-ch sp, ch1, 2tr in last 1-ch sp, join with a sl st in 3rd of 4-ch.
Cont in patt as set, working 3tr in each 1-ch sp and (3tr, 2ch, 3tr) in each 2-ch sp, using foll colour sequence:
  Yarn B for 1 round.
  Yarn C for 1 round.
  Yarn B for 2 rounds.
  Yarn D for 1 round.
  Yarn B for 2 rounds.
  Yarn A for 1 round.
  Yarn B for 2 rounds.
  Yarn C for 1 round.
  Yarn B for 2 rounds.
  Yarn D for 1 round.
  Yarn B for 2 rounds.
  Yarn A for 2 rounds.
  Yarn B for 2 rounds.
  Yarn C for 2 rounds.
  Yarn B for 2 rounds.
  Yarn D for 2 rounds.
  Yarn B for 1 round.
  Yarn A for 1 round.
Fasten off.

Tips

This design can be made to fit any size square cushion. To ensure that your cushion cover is going to be large enough, place the pad in the centre of the crocheted square and fold it around – this will show whether you need to work a few more rounds.

Securing the cover when the bulky cushion is inside is a little awkward, so try folding and seaming one side before slipping the cushion pad inside and completing.

Making up and finishing

Weave in all ends and block as desired to neaten.
Place the granny square WS up and position the cushion pad in the centre, with the straight edges facing towards the points of the square. Fold the points of the granny square in towards the centre of the cushion pad and crochet the four seams together using yarn A, working 1dc in each tr and ch sp.
Fasten off and weave in any ends.

ALL THE
Colours Mandala

Create a colourful boho-style mandala cushion by working with leftover yarns from your stash. Note that this project only uses a small amount of each of the colours listed.

SKILL RATING: ● ● ●

MATERIALS
Cascade 220 (100% Peruvian highland wool, approx. 200m/220yd per 100g/3½oz ball) Aran (worsted) weight yarn:
  1 ball each of shades:
    Nectarine 2451 (A)
    Goldenrod 7827 (B)
    Aqua 8951 (C)
    Natural 8010 (D)
    Purple Hyacinth 7808 (E)
    Deep Lavender 8762 (F)
    Chartreuse 7814 (G)
    Blaze 9542 (H)
    Aspen Heather 8011 (I)
    Blue Hawaii 9421 (J)
    Tiger Lily 9605 (K)

Lion Brand Pound of Love (100% acrylic, approx. 932m/ 1019yd per 454g/16oz ball) Aran (worsted) weight yarn:
  1 ball of shade White 100 (L)

5.5mm (US size I/9) hook

Yarn needle

70cm (28in) diameter cushion pad

FINISHED MEASUREMENTS
Finished cushion is 72cm (28½in) in diameter

TENSION (GAUGE)
13 tr x 7 rounds = 10cm (4in) using a 5.5mm (US size I/9) hook.

ABBREVIATIONS
See page 9.

SPECIAL ABBREVIATION
PS (puff stitch) – *yrh, insert hook into sp, yrh, draw yarn through, keeping yarn loops long; rep from * 5 more times, yrh, draw yarn through all loops on hook, ch1 to close st

For the cushion

FRONT

Using a 5.5mm (US size I/9) hook and yarn A, make a magic ring.

Round 1: Ch4 (counts as 1tr and ch1), *1tr into the ring, ch1; rep from * 10 more times, join with a sl st in 3rd of 3-ch. *12 tr + twelve 1-ch sps.*

Round 2: Change to yarn B, ch2, *PS in next ch sp, ch3; rep from * to end, join with a sl st in top of first PS. *12 PS + twelve 3-ch sps.*

Round 3: Join yarn C in any 3-ch sp, ch3 (counts as 1tr), 2tr in same ch sp, ch1, *3tr in next ch sp, ch1; rep from * to end, join with a sl st in 3rd of 3-ch. *Twelve 3-tr groups + twelve 1-ch sps.*

Round 4: Join yarn D in any 1-ch sp, ch6 (counts as 1tr and ch3), *1tr in next ch sp, ch3; rep from * to end, join with a sl st in 3rd of 6-ch. *12 tr + twelve 3-ch sps.*

Round 5: Join yarn E in any 3-ch sp, ch3 (counts as 1tr), (1tr, ch1, 2tr) in same ch sp, ch1, *(2tr, ch1, 2tr) in next ch sp, ch1; rep from * to end, join with a sl st in 3rd of 3-ch. *48 tr + twenty-four 1-ch sps.*

Round 6: Join yarn F in any 1-ch sp, rep row 3. *Twenty-four 3-tr groups + twenty-four 1-ch sps.*

Round 7: Join yarn C in any 1-ch sp, rep row 4. *24 tr + twenty-four 3-ch sps.*

You can mix and match different yarns from your stash, but to ensure that you get a neat finish try to select yarns of the same weight, as this will help you to maintain an even tension.

MAKE IT YOURS/ The mandala can be worked in any colours you choose; remember that the larger the circle gets the more yarn you will need.

Round 8: Join yarn L in any 3-ch sp, ch3 (counts as 1tr), (2tr, ch1, 3tr) in same ch sp, *(3tr, ch1, 3tr) in next ch sp; rep from * to end, join with a sl st in 3rd of 3-ch. *Forty-eight 3-tr groups + forty-eight 1-ch sps.*

Round 9: Join yarn B in any 1-ch sp, ch3 (counts as 1tr), 2tr in same 1-ch sp, *ch1, 3tr in sp between next two 3-tr groups, ch1, 3tr in next 1-ch sp; rep from * to last two 3-tr groups, ch1, 3tr in sp between last two 3-tr groups, ch1, join with a sl st in 3rd of 3-ch. *Forty-eight 3-tr groups + forty-eight 1-ch sps.*

Round 10: Join yarn G in any 1-ch sp, rep row 2. *48 PS + forty-eight 3-ch sps.*

Round 11: Join yarn H in any 3-ch sp, rep row 3. *Forty-eight 3-tr groups + forty-eight 1-ch sps.*

Round 12: Join yarn F in any 1-ch sp, rep row 4. *48 tr + forty-eight 3-ch sps.*

Round 13: Join yarn I in any 3-ch sp, ch3 (counts as 1tr), 4tr in same ch sp, *5tr in next 3-ch sp; rep from * to end, join with a sl st in 3rd of 3-ch. *240 tr.*

Round 14: Change to yarn D, ch1 (does not count as st), 1dc in each tr to end, join with a sl st in first dc. *240 dc.*

Round 15: Change to yarn J, ch3 (counts as 1tr), 1tr in each dc to end, join with a sl st in 3rd of 3-ch. *240 tr.*

Round 16: Change to yarn B, ch1 (does not count as st), *1dc, ch6, miss next 4 dc; rep from * to end, join with a sl st in first dc. *48 dc + forty-eight 6-ch sps.*

Round 17: Join yarn G in 3rd ch of any 6-ch sp, ch1, 1dc in same ch, *ch7, 1dc in 3rd ch of next 6-ch sp; rep from * to end, ch7, join with a sl st in first dc. *48 dc + forty-eight 7-ch sps.*

Round 18: Join yarn K in any 7-ch sp, ch3 (counts as 1tr), 6tr in same ch sp, *7tr in next ch sp; rep from * to end, join with a sl st in 3rd of 3-ch. *336 tr.*

Round 19: Change to yarn C, ch3 (counts as 1tr), 1tr in each tr to end, join with a sl st in 3rd of 3-ch. *336 tr.* Break yarn, leaving a long end to join to back.

BACK

Using a 5.5mm (US size I/9) hook and yarn L, make a magic ring.

Round 1: Ch3 (counts as 1tr throughout), 1tr into the ring, [ch1, 2tr into the ring] 5 times, ch1, join with a sl st in 3rd of 3-ch. *Six 2-tr groups.*

Round 2: Sl st in next st, sl st in ch sp, ch3, (1tr, ch1, 2tr) in same sp as sl st, *ch1, (2tr, ch1, 2tr) in next sp; rep from * to end of round, ch1, join with a sl st in 3rd of 3-ch. *Twelve 2-tr groups.*

Round 3: Sl st in next st, sl st in ch sp, ch4 (counts as 1tr and ch1 throughout), 3tr in next ch sp, *ch1, 3tr in next ch sp; rep from * to end of round, ch1, 2tr in same ch sp as first sl st, join with a sl st in 3rd of 4-ch. *Twelve 3-tr groups.*

Round 4: Sl st in ch sp, ch3, 2tr in same sp, *ch1, 3tr in next ch sp; rep from * to end of round, ch1, join with a sl st in 3rd of 3-ch.

Round 5 (inc): Ch4, *(3tr, ch1, 3tr) in next ch sp, ch1; rep from * to last ch sp, (3tr, ch1, 2tr) in last ch sp, join with a sl st in 3rd of 4-ch. *Twenty-four 3-tr groups.*

Round 6: Rep round 4.

Round 7: Ch4, 3tr in next ch sp, *ch1, 3tr in next ch sp; rep from * to last ch sp, 2tr in last ch sp, join with a sl st in 3rd of 4-ch.

Round 8: Rep round 4.

Round 9: Rep round 7.

Round 10 (inc): Sl st in ch sp, ch3, 2tr in same sp, *ch1, (3tr, ch1, 3tr) in next ch sp, ch1, 3tr in next ch sp; rep from * to end of round, ch1, join with a sl st in 3rd of 3-ch. *Thirty-six 3-tr groups.*

Cont in patt as set, working inc round every 5th round (working one more 3-tr group between (3tr, ch1, 3tr) increases on every inc round) until work measures 71cm (28in) in diameter.

FOR THE BORDER

Round 1: Ch1, 1dc in each st and ch sp to end, join with a sl st in first dc.

Round 2: Ch1, 1dc in each dc to end, join with a sl st in first dc.

Fasten off.

Making up and finishing

Weave in all ends.
Place front and back pieces WS together with cushion pad sandwiched inside.

Round 1: Using a 5.5mm (US size I/9) hook and yarn C, working through both layers, 1dc in each st to end, join with a sl st in first dc.
Fasten off and weave in ends.

Tip

If you don't have a round cushion pad you can get a piece of foam cut to size – many craft stores offer this service.

CHAPTER TWO

WARM *and Rich*

DARK *Star*

Combining a series of increases and decreases while working in the round creates this striking star motif. Work in a gradient of colours for the most dramatic finish.

SKILL RATING: ● ● ●

MATERIALS
Berroco Comfort (50% nylon, 50% acrylic, approx. 193m/211yd per 100g/3½oz ball) Aran (worsted) weight yarn:
  1 ball each of shades:
    Chalk 9700 (A)
    Buttercup 9712 (B)
  2 balls each of shades:
    Goldenrod 9743 (C)
    Persimmon 9783 (D)
  3 balls each of shades:
    Chianti 9782 (E)
    Dried Plum 9780 (F)

5mm (US size H/8) hook

Yarn needle

Locking stitch markers/safety pins (optional)

FINISHED MEASUREMENTS
Finished throw measures 102cm (40in) square along each spine (from centre to point)

TENSION (GAUGE)
12 tr x 7 rows = 10cm (4in) square, using 5mm (US size H/8) hook.

ABBREVIATIONS
See page 9.

For the throw

Using a 5mm (US size H/8) hook and yarn A, make a magic ring.

Round 1: Ch6 (counts as 1tr and ch3), *1tr into the ring, ch3; rep from * 3 more times, join with a sl st in 3rd of 6-ch. *5 tr + five 3-ch sps.*

Round 2: Sl st in next ch sp, ch3 (counts as 1tr), (2tr, ch2, 3tr) in same ch sp, *(3tr, ch2, 3tr) in next ch sp; rep from * 3 more times, join with a sl st in 3rd of 3-ch. *30 tr + five 2-ch sps.*

Round 3: Sl st in next st, ch3 (counts as 1tr), 1tr in next st, *(3tr, ch2, 3tr) in next ch sp, 1tr in each of next 2 sts, miss 2 sts, 1tr in each of next 2 sts; rep from * 4 more times, miss last st, join with a sl st in 3rd of 3-ch. *50 tr + five 3-ch sps.*

Round 4: Sl st in next st, ch3 (counts as 1tr), 1tr in each of next 3 sts, *(3tr, ch2, 3tr) in next ch sp, 1tr in each of next 4 sts, miss 2 sts, 1tr in each of next 4 sts; rep from * 4 more times, miss last st, join with a sl st in 3rd of 3-ch. *70 tr + five 3-ch sps.*

Tip

Using a magic ring at the centre of the throw means that the yarn can be drawn up, closing the hole at the centre for a neat finish.

MAKE IT YOURS / You can increase the size of this throw by continuing in the pattern as set, but you will need to adjust the yarn quantities accordingly.

Tip

You can using locking stitch markers to help you to keep track of the increases and decreases as you work each round.

Round 5: Sl st in next st, ch3 (counts as 1tr), 1tr in each of next 5 sts, *(3tr, ch2, 3tr) in next ch sp, 1tr in each of next 6 sts, miss 2 sts, 1tr in each of next 6 sts; rep from * 4 more times, miss last st, join with a sl st in 3rd of 3-ch. *90 tr + five 3-ch sps*.

Round 6: Sl st in next st, ch3 (counts as 1tr), 1tr in each of next 7 sts, *(3tr, ch2, 3tr) in next ch sp, 1tr in each of next 8 sts, miss 2 sts, 1tr in each of next 8 sts; rep from * 4 more times, miss last st, join with a sl st in 3rd of 3-ch. *110 tr + five 3-ch sps*.

Cont in patt as set using foll colour sequence:

  Yarn B for 1 round
  Yarn A for 1 round.
  Yarn B for 5 rounds.
  Yarn C for 1 round.
  Yarn B for 1 round.
  Yarn C for 5 rounds.
  Yarn D for 1 round.
  Yarn C for 1 round.
  Yarn D for 5 rounds.
  Yarn E for 1 round.
  Yarn D for 1 round.
  Yarn E for 5 rounds.
  Yarn F for 1 round.
  Yarn E for 1 round.
  Yarn F for 5 rounds.

FOR THE BORDER

Round 1: Cont in yarn F, ch1, 1dc in each st and 2dc in each ch sp to end, join with a sl st in first dc.

Round 2: Ch1, 1dc in each st to end, join with a sl st in first dc.

Fasten off.

Making up and finishing

Weave in all ends and block as desired to neaten.

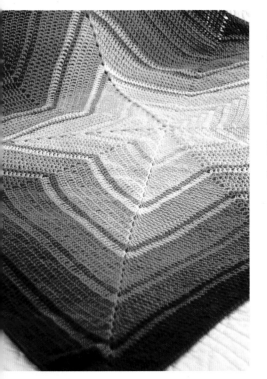

COUNTRY *Colours*

Make your own classic-style blanket using a variation of the granny square to create stripes. Work in a selection of colours for more impact.

SKILL RATING:

MATERIALS
Rowan Summerlite DK (100% cotton, approx. 130m/142yd per 50g/3½oz ball) DK (light worsted) weight yarn:
  5 balls of shade Linen 460 (A)
  4 balls each of shades:
    Mushroom 454 (B)
    Mocha 451 (C)
    Pear 463 (D)
    Khaki 461 (E)
    Cantaloupe 456 (F)

4mm (US size G/6) hook

Yarn needle

FINISHED MEASUREMENTS
Finished blanket is 112 x 190cm (44 x 75in)

TENSION (GAUGE)
Five 3-tr groups x 7 rows = 10cm (4in) square, using 4mm (US size G/6) hook.

ABBREVIATIONS
See page 9.

For the blanket

Using a 4mm (US size G/6) hook and yarn A, work a foundation ch of 152 sts.
Row 1: 1dc in 2nd ch from hook, 1dc in each ch to end.
151 dc.
Row 2: Ch3 (counts as 1tr throughout), 1tr in st at base of 3-ch, *miss 2 sts, 3tr in next st; rep from * to last 3 sts, miss 2 sts, 2tr in last st.
Row 3: Ch3, 3tr in each sp between tr groups on previous row, 1tr in 3rd of 3-ch in previous row.
Row 4: Join in yarn B, ch3, 1tr in sp between last 1tr and 3tr of previous row, 3tr in each sp between tr groups on previous row to last sp, 2tr in last sp.

Row 5: Ch3, 3tr in each sp between tr groups on previous row, 1tr in 3rd of 3-ch in previous row.
Rows 4 and 5 form patt. Cont in patt as set using foll colour sequence:
  Yarn C for 2 rows.
  Yarn D for 2 rows.
  Yarn E for 2 rows.
  Yarn F for 2 rows
Then cont in patt as set, working colour sequence as foll 13 times (so 14 times in total):
  Yarn A for 2 rows.
  Yarn B for 2 rows.
  Yarn C for 2 rows.
  Yarn D for 2 rows.
  Yarn E for 2 rows.
  Yarn F for 2 rows.
Next row: Using yarn F, ch3, miss 3tr, 1dc in next sp, *ch2, 1dc in next sp, rep from * to last tr group, ch3, miss 3tr, 1dc in 3rd of 3-ch in previous row.
Fasten off.

FOR THE BORDER

Round 1: Join in yarn A, ch1, work a dc border around entire edge of work, working 1dc in each stitch and ch along top and bottom edges, approx. 2dc in each row end and (1dc, ch1, 1dc) in each corner, join with a sl st in first dc.
Fasten off.

Making up and finishing

Weave in all ends, and block as desired to neaten.

Changing yarn colour so frequently leaves lots of ends to weave in; hold the ends of the yarn against the work as you change colour, and work the stitches to secure the ends as you go.

When working the border, be sure to maintain an even tension to keep the edges of the blanket flat.

PURPLE *Patch*

This delicate design is created by working around the square from the centre outwards, each row building on the shape of the shell design – play this up by working in bold stripes of colour.

SKILL RATING: ● ● ●

MATERIALS
Rowan Cotton Glacé (100% cotton, approx. 115m/125yd per 50g/1¾oz ball) DK (light worsted) weight yarn:
  3 balls each of shades:
    Oyster 730 (A)
    Rose 861 (B)
    Blood Orange 445 (C)
    Precious 867 (D)
    Winsor 849 (E)
    Ivy 812 (F)

4mm (US size G/6) hook

Yarn needle

FINISHED MEASUREMENTS
Finished blanket is 102cm (40in) square

TENSION (GAUGE)
First 5 rounds measure 10cm (4in) square, using 4mm (US size G/6) hook.

ABBREVIATIONS
See page 9.

SPECIAL ABBREVIATIONS
Make shell – (4tr, ch2, picot, 4tr) in ch sp

Picot – ch2, sl st in first ch

For the blanket

Using a 4mm (US size G/6) hook and yarn A, make a magic ring.
Round 1: Ch4 (counts as 1tr and ch1 throughout), *1tr into the ring, ch1; rep from * 6 more times, ch1, join with a sl st in 3rd of 4-ch. *8 tr + eight 1-ch sps.*
Round 2: Ch1, *1dc in next ch sp, make shell in next ch sp; rep from * 3 more times, join with a sl st in first dc. *4 shells + 4 dc.*
Round 3: Ch4, (1tr, ch3, 1tr, ch1, 1tr) in first dc, *ch4, miss shell, (1tr, ch1, 1tr, ch3, 1tr, ch1, 1tr) in next dc for corner; rep from * twice more, ch4, sl st in 3rd of 4-ch.
Round 4: Ch3 (counts as 1tr throughout), (3tr, ch2, picot, 4tr) in first 1-ch sp, 1dc in next 3-ch sp for corner, make shell in next 1-ch sp, *1dc in 4-ch sp, make shell in next 1-ch sp, 1dc in next 3-ch sp for corner, make shell in next 1-ch sp; rep from * twice more, 1dc in last 4-ch sp, join with a sl st in 3rd of 3-ch, turn, sl st in dc just worked, turn.
Round 5: Ch4, 1tr in same st, ch4, miss shell, *(1tr, ch1, 1tr, ch3, 1tr, ch1, 1tr) in next corner dc for corner, ch4, miss shell, (1tr, ch1, 1tr) in next dc, ch4, miss shell; rep from * to last corner dc, (1tr, ch1, 1tr, ch3, 1tr, ch1, 1tr) in last corner dc for corner, ch4, miss last shell, join with a sl st in 3rd of 4-ch.

MAKE IT YOURS / For a more subtle finish, select one or two tonal shades and work in an ombré style.

Round 6: Change to yarn B, ch3, (3tr, ch2, picot, 4tr) in first 1-ch sp, 1dc in 4-ch sp, *make shell in next 1-ch sp, 1dc in 3-ch sp for corner, make shell in next 1-ch sp, 1dc in 4-ch sp, make shell in next 1-ch sp, 1dc in 4-ch sp; rep from * to last corner, make shell in next 1-ch sp, 1dc in 3-ch sp for corner, make shell in next 1-ch sp, 1dc in last 4-ch sp, join with a sl st 3rd of 3-ch, turn, sl st in dc just worked, turn.

Round 7: Ch4, 1tr in same st, *[ch4, miss shell, (1tr, ch1, 1tr) in next dc] to corner, ch4, miss shell, (1tr, ch1, 1tr, ch3, 1tr, ch1, 1tr) in corner dc for corner; rep from * 3 more times, ch4, join with a sl st in 3rd of 4-ch.

Round 8: Ch3, (3tr, ch2, picot, 4tr) in first 1-ch sp, *[1dc in 4-ch sp, make shell in next 1-ch sp] to corner 3-ch sp, 1dc in 3-ch sp corner, make shell st in next 1-ch sp; rep from * 3 more times, 1dc in 4-ch sp, join with a sl st in 3rd of 3-ch, turn, sl st in dc just worked, turn.

Round 9: Ch4, 1tr in same st, *[ch4, miss shell, (1tr, ch1, 1tr) in next dc] to corner, ch4, miss shell, (1tr, ch1, 1tr, ch3, 1tr, ch1, 1tr) in corner dc for corner; rep from * 3 more times, ch4, join with a sl st in 3rd of 4-ch.

Rounds 8 to 9 form patt, cont in patt as set using foll colour sequence:

Yarn C for 4 rounds.
Yarn D for 4 rounds.
Yarn E for 4 rounds.
Yarn F for 8 rounds.
Yarn E for 4 rounds.
Yarn D for 4 rounds.
Yarn C for 4 rounds.
Yarn B for 4 rounds.
Yarn A for 3 rounds.
Fasten off.

Making up and finishing

Weave in all ends and block as desired to neaten.

Blocking the blanket will help to make a feature of the picot stitches on the shell motifs.

Weave in the ends as neatly as possible to give a professional finish.

WINTER *Pansies*

The traditional style of the granny square is worked in rows here, with increases and decreases to create a dramatic chevron effect.

MATERIALS
Bernat Super Value (100% acrylic, approx. 389m/425yd per 200g/7oz ball) Aran (worsted) weight yarn:
  1 ball each of shades:
    White 07391 (A)
    Bright Teal 53202 (B)
    Lilac 53317 (C)
    Magenta 53402 (D)
    Aqua 53201 (E)
5.5mm (US size I/9) hook

Locking stitch marker/safety pin (optional)

Yarn needle

FINISHED MEASUREMENTS
Finished blanket is 94 x 152cm (37 x 60in)

TENSION (GAUGE)
Four and a half 3-tr clusters x 5 rows = 10cm (4in) square, using 5.5mm (US size I/9) hook.

ABBREVIATIONS
See page 9.

For the blanket

Using a 5.5mm (US size I/9) hook and yarn A, work a foundation ch of 143 sts.

Row 1: 3tr in 6th ch from hook (missed 5-ch counts as 1tr and missed 2 ch), *[miss 2 ch, 3tr in next ch] 3 times, ch2, 3tr in next ch, [miss 2 ch, 3tr in next ch] 3 times, miss 3 ch, 3tr in next ch; rep from * to end, finishing last repeat with miss 2 ch, 1tr in last ch. *Forty-eight 3-tr clusters.*

Row 2: Change to yarn B, ch3 (counts as 1tr throughout), *[3tr in next sp between clusters] 3 times, (3tr, ch2, 3tr) in next 2-ch sp, [3tr in next sp between clusters] 3 times, miss 1 sp; rep from * to last st, 1tr in last st.

Row 3: Change to yarn C, ch3, *[3tr in next sp between clusters] 3 times, (3tr, ch2, 3tr) in next 2-ch sp, [3tr in next sp between clusters] 3 times, miss 1 sp; rep from * to last st, 1tr in last st.

MAKE IT YOURS / Create thicker stripes by working more rows in each shade before changing to the next colour yarn.

Row 4: Change to yarn D, ch3, *[3tr in next sp between clusters] 3 times, (3tr, ch2, 3tr) in next 2-ch sp, [3tr in next sp between clusters] 3 times, miss 1 sp; rep from * to last st, 1tr in last st.
Row 5: Change to yarn E, ch3, *[3tr in next sp between clusters] 3 times, (3tr, ch2, 3tr) in next 2-ch sp, [3tr in next sp between clusters] 3 times, miss 1 sp; rep from * to last st, 1tr in last st.
Row 6: Change to yarn A, ch3, *[3tr in next sp between clusters] 3 times, (3tr, ch2, 3tr) in next 2-ch sp, [3tr in next sp between clusters] 3 times, miss 1 sp; rep from * to last st, 1tr in last st.
Rows 2 to 6 form patt, cont in patt as set until work measures 152cm (60in), ending after a yarn A row.
Fasten off.

FOR THE BORDER

Round 1: With RS facing, using a 5.5mm (US size I/9) hook, join yarn E in first st after top right corner, ch1, *1dc in each st to next corner, (1dc, ch1, 1dc) in corner, 2dc in each row end to corner, (1dc, ch1, 1dc) in corner; rep from * once more, join with a sl st in first dc.
Round 2: Ch1, *1dc in each st to next corner, (1dc, ch1, 1dc) in corner sp; rep from * 3 more times, 1dc in each st to end, join with a sl st in first dc.
Fasten off.

Making up and finishing

Weave in all ends and block as desired to neaten.

You can use a locking stitch marker to mark out the third stitch in the chain, to help you see where to insert the hook at the end of the next row.

Adding the border is a great way to keep the sides of the blanket neat — be sure to keep the yarn joins flush to the work to keep the border even.

Waves OF COLOUR

Working with simple increasing and decreasing creates a repeated ripple pattern across this blanket. Select a combination of tonal colours to play up the design.

SKILL RATING: ● ● ●

MATERIALS
Berroco Modern Cotton (60% cotton, 40% synthetic, approx. 191m/209yd per 100g/3½oz ball) Aran (worsted) weight yarn:
  2 balls each of shades:
    Point Judith 1645 (A)
    Bristol 1658 (B)
    Del 1627 (C)
    Matunuck 1652 (D)
    Piper 1603 (E)

5.5mm (US size I/9) hook

Yarn needle

FINISHED MEASUREMENTS
Finished blanket is 106 x 190cm (42 x 75in)

TENSION (GAUGE)
17 tr x 7 rows = 10cm (4in) square in ripple patt, using 5.5mm (US size I/9) hook.

ABBREVIATIONS
See page 9.

For the blanket

Using a 5.5mm (US size I/9) hook and yarn A, work a foundation ch of 154 sts.

Row 1: 1dc in 2nd ch from hook, 1dc in each ch to end. *153 dc.*

Row 2: Ch3 (counts as 1tr throughout), 1tr in same st, 2tr in each of next 2 sts, miss next st, [1tr in next st, miss next st] 5 times, *2tr in each of next 6 sts, miss next st, [1tr in next st, miss next st] 5 times; rep from * to last 3 sts, 2tr in each st to end. *153 tr.*

Row 3: Ch1 (does not count as st throughout), 1dc FLO in each stitch to end. *153 dc FLO.*

Row 4: Ch3, 1tr in same st, 2tr in each of next 2 sts, miss next st, [1tr in next st, miss foll st] 5 times, *2tr in each of next 6 sts, miss next st, [1tr in next st, miss foll st] 5 times; rep from * to last 3 sts, 2tr in each st to end. *153 tr.*

Tips

You can use locking stitch markers to help keep your place in the pattern if needed.

Holding the yarn against the work to secure it when you change colours will save time weaving ends in when finishing the blanket.

Row 5: Ch1, 1dc FLO in each st to end. *153 dc FLO.*
Rows 2–5 form patt, cont in pattern as set in foll colour sequence:
Yarn B for 4 rows.
Yarn C for 4 rows.
Yarn D for 4 rows.
Yarn E for 4 rows.
Yarn A for 4 rows.
Cont until work measures 190cm (75in), ending after 4 rows in yarn E.
Fasten off.

Making up and finishing

Weave in all ends and block as desired to neaten.

MAKE IT YOURS / You can create wider stripes by simply working the four-row repeat more times in each colour.

SPIKES AND *Stripes*

This surface design is created by working into previous rows to give different lengths of spikes – it is a surprisingly simple technique.

SKILL RATING: ● ◐ ◐

MATERIALS
Lion Brand 24/7 Cotton (100% cotton, approx. 170m/186yd per 100g/3½oz ball) Aran (worsted) weight yarn:
  4 balls each of shades:
    Jade 178 (A)
    Goldenrod 158 (B)
    Mint 156 (C)

5mm (US size H/8) hook

Yarn needle

FINISHED MEASUREMENTS
Finished blanket is 66 x 140cm (26 x 55in)

TENSION (GAUGE)
13 dc x 15 rows = 10cm (4in) square in double crochet, using 5mm (US size H/8) hook.

ABBREVIATIONS
See page 9.

SPECIAL ABBREVIATION
Spike st (spike stitch) – insert hook through next st on specified row below, then work a double crochet

For the throw

Using a 5mm (US size H/8) hook and yarn A, work a foundation ch of 62 sts.
Row 1: 1dc in 2nd ch from hook, 1dc in each st to end. *61 dc.*
Rows 2–6: Ch1 (does not count as st throughout), 1dc in each st to end.

Tips

Carry the yarns against the work when you change colour to save time weaving the ends in when finishing the project.

Try to maintain the tension as you create the long spike stitches, so as not to gather up the work.

Row 7: Change to yarn B, ch1, 1dc in first st, *Spike st in 2nd row below, Spike st in 3rd row below, Spike st in 4th row below, Spike st in 3rd row below, Spike st in 2nd row below, 1dc in next st; rep from * to end.
Rows 8–12: Ch1, 1dc in each st to end.
Row 13: Change to yarn C, ch1, 1dc in first st, *Spike st in 2nd row below, Spike st in 3rd row below, Spike st in 4th row below, Spike st in 3rd row below, Spike st in 2nd row below, 1dc in next st; rep from * to end.
Rows 14–18: Ch1, 1dc in each st to end.
Row 19: Change to yarn A, ch1, 1dc in first st, *Spike st in 2nd row below, Spike st in 3rd row below, Spike st in 4th row below, Spike st in 3rd row below, Spike st in 2nd row below, 1dc in next st; rep from * to end.
Rows 20–24: Ch1, 1dc in each st to end.
Cont in patt as set until work measures 140cm (55in).
Fasten off.

Making up and finishing

Weave in all ends and block as desired to neaten.

MAKE IT YOURS / Create your own surface design by alternating the length at which you work the long spike stitches.

$\mathcal{B}eehive$ BLANKET

Hexagons never go out of style. Work with modern shades to create your own dramatic design.

SKILL RATING: ● ◐ ◐

MATERIALS

Brown Sheep Company Lamb's Pride Worsted (85% wool, 15% mohair, approx. 173m/189yd per 113g/4oz ball) Aran (worsted) weight yarn:
  2 balls each of shades:
    Sunburst Gold M14 (A)
    Autumn Harvest M22 (B)
    Turquoise Depths M187 (C)
  1 ball of shade Blue Flannel M82 (D)
Caron Simply Soft (100% acrylic, approx. 288m/315yd per 170g/6oz ball) Aran (worsted) weight yarn:
  1 ball of shade White 9701 (E)
5.5mm (US size I/9) hook

FINISHED MEASUREMENTS

Finished blanket is 91.5 x 117cm (36 x 46in)

TENSION (GAUGE)

12 tr sts x 6 rows = 10cm (4in), using 5.5mm (US size I/9) hook.

ABBREVIATIONS

See page 9.

For the blanket

HEXAGON

Using a 5.5mm (US size I/9) hook and yarn A, make a magic ring.
Round 1: Ch3 (counts as 1tr throughout), 1tr into the ring, ch2, *2tr into the ring, ch2; rep from * 4 more times, join with a sl st in 3rd of 3-ch. *12 tr.*
Round 2: Ch3, 1tr in next st, *(1tr, ch2, 1tr) in next ch sp, 1tr in each of next 2 sts; rep from * 4 more times, (1tr, ch2, 1tr) in last ch sp, join with a sl st in 3rd of 3-ch. *24 tr.*
Round 3: Ch3, 1tr in each of next 2 sts, *(1tr, ch2, 1tr) in next ch sp, 1tr in each of next 4 sts; rep from * 4 more times, (1tr, ch2, 1tr) in last ch-sp, 1tr in next st, join with a sl st in 3rd of 3-ch. *36 tr.*
Round 4: Ch3, 1tr in each of next 3 sts, *(1tr, ch2, 1tr) in next ch sp, 1tr in each of next 6 sts; rep from * 4 more times, (1tr, ch2, 1tr) in last ch sp, 1tr in each of next 2 sts, join with a sl st in 3rd of 3-ch. *48 tr.*
Round 5: Ch3, 1tr in each of next 4 sts, *(1tr, ch2, 1tr) in next ch sp, 1tr in each of next 8 sts; rep from * 4 more times, (1tr, ch2, 1tr) in last ch sp, 1tr in each of next 3 sts, join with a sl st in 3rd of 3-ch. *60 tr.*
Fasten off.
Rep to make 12 hexagons in yarn A, 12 hexagons in yarn B, 11 hexagons in yarn C and 7 hexagons in yarn D, 42 hexagons in total.

Making up and finishing

Weave in all ends and block as desired to neaten.
Arrange the hexagons into six rows of seven blocks in desired design.
Using a 5.5mm (US size I/9) hook and yarn E, working through both layers, work through the back loops only and join with 1dc in each st.

Tips The centre of each hexagon is made with a magic ring; be sure to draw these up fully to close the hole for a neater finish.

When joining, arrange the pieces as desired and try to work in long continuous lines to avoid having lots of extra ends to sew in.

MAKE IT YOURS / Work with an even number of each colour hexagon and arrange to create your own geometric design.

AUTUMN *Leaves*

Granny stripes are a firm favourite – transform this classic crochet panel into a cosy cushion cover.

MATERIALS

Berroco Comfort (50% nylon, 50% acrylic, approx. 193m/210yd per 100g/3½oz ball) Aran (worsted) weight yarn:
  3 balls of shade Chalk 9700 (A)
  1 ball each of shades:
    Sprig 9721 (B)
    Pumpkin 9724(C)
    Hummus 9720 (D)

5mm (US size H/8) and 5.5mm (US size I/9) hooks

Yarn needle

63cm (25in) square cushion pad

3 buttons, 2cm (¾in) diameter

FINISHED MEASUREMENTS

Finished cushion is 63cm (25in) square

TENSION (GAUGE)

8 tr clusters (incl tr worked in spaces on foll row) x 7 rows = 10cm (4in), using 5mm (US size H/8) hook.

ABBREVIATIONS

See page 9.

For the cushion

Using a 5mm (US size H/8) hook and yarn A, work a foundation ch of 74 sts.

Row 1: 1dc in 2nd ch from hook, 1dc in each ch to end. *73 dc.*

Row 2: Ch3 (counts as 1tr throughout), 1tr in st at base of 3-ch, *miss 2 sts, 3tr in next st; rep from * to last 3 sts, miss 2 sts, 2tr in last st. *73 tr.*

Row 3: Change to yarn B, ch3, 3tr in each sp between tr groups on previous row, 1tr in 3rd of 3-ch in previous row. *74 tr.*

Row 4: Change to yarn A, ch3, 1tr in sp between last 1tr and 3tr on previous row, 3tr in each sp between tr groups on previous row to last sp, 2tr in last sp. *73 tr.*

Row 5: Change to yarn C, ch3, 3tr in each sp between tr groups on previous row, 1tr in 3rd of 3-ch on previous row. *74 tr.*

Rows 4 and 5 form patt. Cont in patt as set using foll colour sequence, beginning with yarn A:

Yarn A for 1 row.
Yarn D for 1 row.
Yarn A for 1 row.
Yarn B for 1 row.
Yarn A for 1 row.
Yarn C for 1 row.

Cont in patt as set until work measures 114cm (45in), ending with a yarn A row.

Fasten off.

MAKE IT YOURS/ Change the tone of this make by switching the white yarn for a darker shade, like grey or black.

Sew on the buttons securely; if your yarn needle doesn't pass easily through the button's hole, try using a needle and matching sewing cotton instead.

Changing yarn colour so frequently leaves lots of ends to weave in; hold the ends of the yarn against the work as you change colour, and work the stitches to secure the ends as you go.

FOR THE BORDER

Round 1: With RS facing, using a 5.5mm (US size I/9) hook, join yarn A in first st after first corner of either long side, ch1, work a dc border around entire edge of work, working approx. 2dc in each row end, 1dc in each stitch and ch along top and bottom edges, and (1dc, ch1, 1dc) in each corner, join with a sl st in first dc.

Round 2: Ch1, *1dc in each st to next corner, (1dc, ch1, 1dc) in corner; rep from * twice more, create buttonholes as foll: 1dc in each of next 5 sts, ch6, 1dc in each of next 32 sts, ch6, 1dc in each of next 32 sts, ch6, 1dc in each st to next corner, (1dc, ch1, 1dc) in corner, join with a sl st in first dc.

Fasten off.

Making up and finishing

Weave in all ends and block as desired to neaten.
With WS facing, fold crochet panel in half, aligning two shorter edges, and join two side seams by working 1dc in each st, working through both layers.
Fasten off.
Sew on buttons to correspond with buttonholes.

ORANGE *Juice*

Bobble stitch is a great way to add a fun and tactile finish to a simple cushion cover. These clever stitches are created by looping the yarn over the hook multiple times and drawing back through, repeating this to create a fantastic texture.

SKILL RATING: ● ● ◉

MATERIALS

Stylecraft Special Aran (100% acrylic, approx. 196m/214yd per 100g/3½oz ball) Aran (worsted) weight yarn:
  5 balls of shade Spice 1711

5.5mm (US size I/9) hook

Yarn needle

63cm (25in) square cushion pad

4 buttons, 2cm (¾in) diameter

FINISHED MEASUREMENTS

Finished cushion is 64cm (25½in) square

TENSION (GAUGE)

12 dc x 14 rows = 10cm (4in) in stitch patt, using 5.5mm (US size I/9) hook.

ABBREVIATIONS

See page 9.

SPECIAL ABBREVIATION

Bobble – yrh, insert hook in st, yrh, draw yarn through st, yrh, draw yarn through first 2 loops (2 loops on hook), *yrh, take hook through st, yrh, draw yarn through st; rep until 10 loops on hook, yrh, draw yarn through all loops

For the cushion

FRONT

Using a 5.5mm (US size I/9) hook, make a foundation ch of 76 sts.
Row 1: 1dc in 2nd ch from hook, 1dc in each ch to end. *75 sts.*
Row 2: Ch1, 1dc in each st to end.
Row 3: Ch1, 1dc in each of first 3 sts, *bobble in next st, 1dc in each of next 3 sts; rep from * to end.
Rows 4–6: Ch1, 1dc in each st to end. *75 sts.*
Row 7: Ch1, 1dc in each of first 5 sts, *bobble in next st, 1dc in each of next 3 sts; rep from * to last 5 sts, 1dc in each of last 5 sts.
Rows 8–10: Ch1, 1dc in each st to end. *75 sts.*
Rows 3 to 10 form patt. Rep them until work measures 63.5cm (25in), ending after a row 3 bobble row.
Next row: Ch1, 1dc in each st to end. *75 sts.*
Rep last row once more.
Buttonhole row: Ch1, 1dc in each of next 15 sts, ch2, miss 2 sts, 1dc in each of next 12 sts, ch2, miss 2 sts, 1dc in each of next 14 sts, ch2, miss 2 sts, 1dc in each of next 12 sts, ch2, miss 2 sts, 1dc in each st to end.
Next row: Ch1, 1dc in each st to end. *75 sts.*
Rep last row twice more.
Fasten off.

BACK

Using a 5.5mm (US size I/9) hook, make a magic ring.
Round 1: Ch3 (counts as 1tr throughout), 2tr into the ring, *ch2, 3tr into the ring; rep from * twice more, ch2, join with a sl st in 3rd of 3-ch.

Round 2: Ch4 (counts as 1tr and ch1 throughout), *(3tr, 2ch, 3tr) in next 2-ch sp, ch1; rep from * twice more, (3tr, ch2, 2tr) in last 2-ch sp, join with a sl st in 3rd of 4-ch.

Round 3: Ch3, 2tr in first 1-ch sp, *ch1, (3tr, ch2, 3tr) in next 2-ch sp, ch1, 3tr in next 1-ch sp; rep from * twice more, ch1, (3tr, ch2, 3tr) in last 2-ch sp, ch1, join with a sl st in 3rd of 3-ch.

Round 4: Ch4, 3tr in first 1-ch sp, *ch1, (3tr, ch2, 3tr) in next 2-ch sp, ch1, 3tr in next 1-ch sp, ch1, 3tr in next 1-ch sp; rep from * twice more, ch1, (3tr, ch2, 3tr) in next 2-ch sp, ch1, 2tr in last 1-ch sp, join with a sl st in 3rd of 4-ch.
Cont in patt as set for a further 15 rounds, or until square measures 63.5cm (25in).

Next round: Ch1, *1dc in each st to corner, (1dc, 1ch, 1dc) in corner; rep from * 4 times, join with a sl st in first dc.
Fasten off.

Making up and finishing

Weave in all ends.
Place front and back panels WS together, with front panel facing and the buttonhole edge at the top. Using a 5.5mm (US size I/9) hook, join in the yarn 10 sts before top left corner, *working through both layers, 1dc in each st to corner, (1dc, ch1, 1dc) in corner; rep from * 3 more times (working 1dc in each row end), (1dc, ch1, 1dc) in last corner, 1dc in each of next 2 sts. Fasten off, leaving opening in top edge for inserting the cushion.
Fasten off.
Sew on buttons to correspond with buttonholes along opening.

Try to maintain the length of the loops when bringing the yarn around the hook, as this will create even bobble stitches.

To find the correct position for the buttons, lay the cover flat and align the top edge. Then use pins to mark the position of the buttons through the buttonholes onto the other side.

MAKE IT YOURS / Create a reversible design by working an additional bobble stitch panel for the back of the cushion. You will need to increase the yarn quantities accordingly.

PARALLEL *Lines*

The surface of a cushion panel made with simple stitches can be embellished by working surface crochet across the right side of the fabric. This cushion makes use of variegated yarns for added contrast.

SKILL RATING:

MATERIALS

Lion Brand Vanna's Choice (100% acrylic, approx. 156m/170yd per 100g/3½oz ball) Aran (worsted) weight yarn:
  2 balls of shade Silver Grey 149 (A)

Lion Brand Landscapes (100% acrylic, approx. 134m/147yd per 100g/3½oz ball) Aran (worsted) weight yarn:
  1 ball of shade Desert Spring 204 (B)

6mm (US size J/10) hook

Yarn needle

63cm (25in) square cushion pad

Cushion cover or fabric to create backing

FINISHED MEASUREMENTS

Finished cushion is 64cm (25½in) square

TENSION (GAUGE)

10 htr x 8 rows = 10cm (4in) square, using 6mm (US size J/10) hook.

ABBREVIATIONS

See page 9.

For the panel

Using a 6mm (US size J/10) hook and yarn A, work a foundation ch of 61 sts.
Row 1: 1htr in 2nd ch from hook, 1htr in each st to end. *60 htr.*
Row 2: Ch2 (does not count as htr), 1 htr in each st to end.
Cont working in rows of htr until work measures 61cm (24in) square.

FOR THE BORDER

Round 1: 1ch, 1dc in each st to corner, (1dc, 1ch, 1dc) in corner; rep from * 4 times, join with a sl st in first dc.
Rounds 2–3: Rep round 1.
Fasten off.

ADD SURFACE CROCHET

Holding yarn on back of crochet panel, pass hook through to catch yarn, bring a loop through to surface. Push hook back through and catch yarn again, bring a loop through to surface and draw through loop on hook as though working a sl st. Rep to create patt of 5 vertical lines intersecting with 5 horizontal lines.

Tips This panel can be stitched onto a pre-made cushion cover, or you can create your own cover in your choice of fabric.

The surface crochet stitches are worked with the yarn held underneath the crochet panel, and drawn up through to the surface.

Making up and finishing

Weave in all ends.
Place panel onto front of fabric cushion cover and stitch to secure.

To create your own fabric backing, cut two pieces of fabric to 45 x 67.5cm (18 x 27in). Fold 2.5cm (1in) to the WS around each side, press and sew in place. Place the two pieces together, both with RS facing up, to create a 62.5cm (25in) square panel – the pieces will overlap in the centre to allow the cushion pad to be inserted. With WS together, place the assembled fabric piece onto the crochet panel and sew around the outer edges.

MAKE IT YOURS / Surface crochet can be used to add any motif you like; experiment with geometric or swirling designs.

PRECIOUS *Metals*

Make a statement cushion with dramatic chevrons, which are created by working increases and decreases across the length of the row.

MATERIALS
Stylecraft Special Chunky (100% acrylic, approx. 144m/157yd per 100g/3½oz ball) chunky (bulky) weight yarn:
- 3 balls of shade Silver 1203 (A)
- 2 balls each of shades:
  - Copper 1029 (B)
  - Graphite 1063 (C)

6mm (US size J/10) hook

Yarn needle

63cm (25in) square cushion pad

4 x buttons, 2.5cm (1in) diameter

Locking stitch markers/safety pins (optional)

FINISHED MEASUREMENTS
Finished cushion is 64cm (25½in) square

TENSION (GAUGE)
10 tr x 6 rows = 10cm (4in) square, using 6mm (US size J/10) hook.

ABBREVIATIONS
See page 9.

SPECIAL ABBREVIATION
tr3tog (treble 3 stitches together) – *yrh, insert hook in next st, yrh, draw yarn through, yrh, draw through first 2 loops on hook; rep from * twice more, yrh, draw through rem 4 loops on hook

For the cushion

Using a 6mm (US size J/10) hook and yarn A, work a foundation ch of 66 sts.

Row 1: 1tr in 3rd ch from hook (missed ch2 does not count as tr), 1tr in each of next 6 sts, 3tr in next st, 1tr in each of next 6 sts, *tr3tog, 1tr in each of next 6 sts, 3tr in next st, 1tr in each of next 6 sts; rep from * to last 2 sts, tr2tog. *64 tr.*

Row 2: Ch3 (does not count as tr), miss first st at base of ch, 1tr in each of next 7 sts, 3tr in next st, 1tr in each of next 6 sts, *tr3tog, 1tr in each of next 6 sts, 3tr in next st, 1tr in each of next 6 sts, rep from * to last 2 sts, tr2tog.

Row 2 forms patt. Change to yarn B and cont in patt as set, working 2 rows in each colour until work measures 146cm (57½in), ending with 2 rows in yarn C.

FOR THE BORDER

Round 1: Beginning at right-hand corner of top edge, using a 6mm (US size J/10) hook and yarn A, ch1, work a dc border around entire edge of work, working 1dc in each tr along top edge, 1dc in each ch along bottom edge, approx. 2dc in each row end and 2dc in each corner, join with a sl st in first dc.

Tips Stitch markers can be used to mark the positions of the increases and decreases along the row.

Hold the ends of the yarn against the work as you change colour and work the stitches to secure the ends as you go.

Buttonhole round: Ch1, *1dc in each dc to chevron point of top edge, ch4, miss next dc; rep from * three more times, 1dc in each dc to end, join with a sl st in first dc. Four buttonhole loops made.
Fasten off.

Making up and finishing

Weave in all ends.
With WS facing, fold bottom edge of chevron panel up by 63.5cm (25in). Hold the side edges of the folded section together and, using a 6mm (US size J/10) and yarn A and working through both layers, work 1dc in each st down side seam to join. Rep for 2nd side seam.
Fold the top edge down by 25cm (10in) for overlapping upper flap and sew four buttons in place to correspond with buttonhole loops.

CHAPTER THREE

NEUTRAL *and Natural*

RIVERBANK *Blanket*

Granny squares are some of the most iconic designs for crochet blankets. This large blanket is worked by alternating a variegated and a solid-colour yarn to create a super-sized design in grassy greens.

SKILL RATING: ● ● ●

MATERIALS
Caron Simply Soft (100% acrylic, approx. 288m/314yd per 170g/6oz ball) Aran (worsted) weight yarn:
  2 balls of shade Off White 9702 (A)

Caron Cakes (80% acrylic, 20% wool, approx. 350m/383yd per 200g/7oz ball) Aran (worsted) weight yarn:
  2 balls of shade Pistachio 17020 (B)

5mm (US size H/8) hook

Yarn needle

FINISHED MEASUREMENTS
Finished blanket is 127cm (50in) square

TENSION (GAUGE)
First 3 rounds measure approx. 11.5cm (4½in) square.

ABBREVIATIONS
See page 9.

For the blanket

Using a 5mm (US size H/8) hook and yarn A, make a magic ring.
Round 1: Ch3 (counts as 1tr), 2tr into the ring, *ch2, 3tr into the ring; rep from * twice more, ch2, join with a sl st in 3rd of 3-ch.
Round 2: Join in yarn B, ch4 (counts as 1tr and ch1) *(3tr, ch2, 3tr) in next 2-ch sp, ch1; rep from * twice more, (3tr, ch2, 2tr) in last 2-ch sp, join with a sl st in 3rd of 4-ch.
Round 3: Change to yarn A, ch3 (counts as 1tr), 2tr in first 1-ch sp, *ch1, (3tr, ch2, 3tr) in next 2-ch sp, ch1, 3tr in next 1-ch sp; rep from * twice more, ch1, (3tr, ch2, 3tr) in last 2-ch sp, ch1, join with a sl st in 3rd of 3-ch.
Round 4: Change to yarn B, ch4 (counts as 1tr and 1ch), 3tr in next 1-ch sp, *ch1, (3tr, ch2, 3tr) in next 2-ch sp, ch1, 3tr in next 1-ch sp, ch1, 3tr in next 1-ch sp; rep from * twice more, ch1, (3tr, ch2, 3tr) in next 2-ch sp, ch1, 2tr in last 1-ch sp, join with a sl st in 3rd of 4-ch.
Cont in patt as set, working 3tr in each 1-ch sp and (3tr, 2ch, 3tr) in each 2-ch sp, for 30 more rounds (34 rounds in total) ending with a yarn B round.

FOR THE BORDER

Round 1: Using a 5mm (US size H/8) hook and yarn B, *1dc in each st and 1-ch sp to corner 2-ch sp, (1dc, ch1, 1dc) in corner 2-ch sp; rep from * 3 more times, 1dc in each st and 1-ch sp to end, join with sl st in first st.
Round 2: Ch1, *1dc in each st to corner ch sp, (1dc, ch1, 1dc) in corner ch sp; rep from * 3 more times, 1dc in each st to end, join with sl st in first st.
Fasten off.

Making up and finishing

Weave in all ends and block as desired to neaten.

MAKE IT YOURS / For a more flamboyant design, create tassels to secure to each corner, or add a length of fringing around the edge.

Tips

Holding the ends of the yarn against the work as you change colour, and working the stitches to secure the ends as you go, will save time when finishing the blanket — and can be more efficient with the yarn!

The magic ring is a neat foundation at the centre of the blanket, but can be a little fiddly to master. See page 116 for instructions; it is worth practising as it can be drawn up neatly to close the hole in the centre completely.

MAKE IT YOURS / Make this without using a hook if you prefer; simply work the stitches using your hands instead!

FIRESIDE *Friend*

Make a striking addition to your interior with this statement design, worked in an ultra-chunky merino yarn. You can throw it over an armchair, or sit on it in front of the fire.

SKILL RATING: ● ● ●

MATERIALS
World of Wool Merino Jumbo Yarn (100% merino wool, approx. 45m/50yd per 1kg/2lb 4oz ball) arm knitting weight yarn:
- 1 ball of shade Terracotta (A)
- 2 balls of shade Flesh (B)
- 3 balls of shade Oyster (C)

25mm (US size U) hook

FINISHED MEASUREMENTS
Finished blanket is approx. 97cm (38¼in) square

TENSION (GAUGE)
Exact tension is not essential in this project.

ABBREVIATIONS
See page 9.

For the rug

Using a 25mm (US size U) hook and yarn A, make a magic ring.
Round 1: Ch3 (counts as 1tr), 2tr into the ring, *ch2, 3tr into the ring; rep from * twice more, ch2, join with a sl st in 3rd of 3-ch.
Round 2: Ch4 (counts as 1tr and ch1), *(3tr, ch2, 3tr) in next 2-ch sp, ch1; rep from * twice more, (3tr, ch2, 2tr) in last 2-ch sp, join with a sl st in 3rd of 3-ch.
Round 3: Change to yarn B, ch3 (counts as 1tr), 2tr in first 1-ch sp, *ch1, (3tr, ch2, 3tr) in next 2-ch sp, ch1, 3tr in next 1-ch sp; rep from * twice more, ch1, (3tr, ch2, 3tr) in last 2-ch sp, ch1, join with a sl st in 3rd of 3-ch.
Round 4: Ch4 (counts as 1tr and ch1), 3tr in next 1-ch sp, *ch1, (3tr, ch2, 3tr) in next 2-ch sp, ch1, 3tr in next 1-ch sp, ch1, 3tr in next 1-ch sp; rep from * twice more, ch1, (3tr, ch2, 3tr) in next 2-ch sp, ch1, 2tr in last 1-ch sp, join with a sl st in 3rd of 4-ch.
Change to yarn C, cont in patt as set, working 3tr in each 1-ch sp and (3tr, 2ch, 3tr) in each 2-ch sp, for 2 more rounds (6 rounds in total).
Fasten off.

Making up and finishing

Weave in all ends and block as desired to neaten.

Tips

This project becomes very heavy, so you might find it easier to lay the work on the sofa or a bed as you crochet.

You won't be able to thread this yarn onto a yarn needle to weave in the ends, so simply use your fingers or the hook to neatly guide the ends in and secure them.

SUMMER *Breeze*

Create a luxurious textured throw with puff stitch. These voluminous stitches, which are surprisingly easy yet very striking, are created by working additional loops of yarn around the hook.

SKILL RATING: ● ● ○

MATERIALS

Caron Simply Soft (100% acrylic, approx. 288m/315yd per 170g/6oz ball) Aran (worsted) weight yarn:
   3 balls of shade Chartreuse 9771 (A)
   6 balls of shade Bone 9703 (B)

5mm (US size H/8) hook

Yarn needle

FINISHED MEASUREMENTS

Finished blanket is 105 x 153cm (42 x 60in)

TENSION (GAUGE)

5.5 sts x 7.5 rows = 10cm (4in) in puff stitch, using 5mm (US size H/8) hook.

ABBREVIATIONS

See page 9.

SPECIAL ABBREVIATION

PS (puff stitch) – *yrh, insert hook in st, yrh, draw yarn through, keeping yarn loops long; rep from * 5 more times, yrh, draw yarn through all loops on hook, ch1 to close st

For the throw

Using a 5mm (US size H/8) hook and yarn A, work a foundation ch of 101 sts.

Row 1: 1PS in 3rd ch from hook (missed ch2 counts as ch sp), ch1, miss next ch, *1PS in next ch, ch1, miss next ch; rep from * to last ch, 1PS in last ch. *50 PS*.

Row 2: Ch2 (counts as ch sp), miss first PS, *1PS in next ch sp, ch1, miss 1 PS, rep from * to last 2-ch sp, 1PS in last 2-ch sp.

Row 2 forms patt. Cont in patt as set until work measures 50cm (20in).

Join in yarn B, cont until work measures 153cm (60in).

Next row: *1dc in next st at top of PS, 1dc in next ch sp; rep from * to end.

Fasten off.

Making up and finishing

Weave in all ends and block as desired to neaten.

 Try to create loops of a similar size when working each puff stitch; this will help to keep the finished piece really neat.

This stitch requires a lot of yarn, so be sure to have the full amount before you begin.

MAKE IT YOURS / Adapt the design by working in stripes of colour rather than a simple colourblock band.

EARTH *Tones*

Nothing is quite as cosy and comforting as this super-chunky blanket. It alternates two rows to create the pattern, so it's ideal for a quick-and-easy project.

SKILL RATING: ● ○ ○

MATERIALS

Rowan Big Wool (100% wool, approx. 80m/87yd per 100g/3½oz ball) super chunky (super bulky) weight yarn:

4 balls each of shades:
    Linen 048 (A)
    Concrete 061 (B)
    Biscotti 082 (C)
    Prize 064 (D)
    Glum 056 (E)

15mm (US size Q) hook

Yarn needle

FINISHED MEASUREMENTS

Finished blanket is 89 x 165cm (35 x 65in)

TENSION (GAUGE)

6 sts x 4 rows = 10cm (4in) square.

ABBREVIATIONS

See page 9.

For the blanket

Using a 15mm (US size Q) hook and yarn A held double, work a foundation ch of 51 sts.

Row 1: 1dc in 2nd ch from hook, 1dc in each ch to end. *50 dc.*

Row 2: Ch3 (counts as 1tr), 1tr in next st, 1tr in each st to end. *50 tr.*

Row 3: Ch1 (does not count as st), 1dc in each st to end. *50 dc.*

Rows 2 and 3 form patt, cont in patt as set, using foll colour sequence:

    Yarn A for 12 more rows, ending on dc row.
    Yarn B for 14 rows, ending on dc row.
    Yarn C for 14 rows, ending on dc row.
    Yarn D for 14 rows, ending on dc row.
    Yarn E for 14 rows, ending on dc row.
Fasten off.

Making up and finishing

Weave in all ends and block as desired to neaten.

Tips

This pattern alternates between a row of double crochet and a row of treble; looking at the row below will help you to work out what you need to work on the current row.

The dense finish is created by holding the yarn double – be sure that you are catching both strands of yarn each time you work a stitch.

SPRING *Crocuses*

Make the most of variegated yarns to add a flash of colour to these circle-centred granny squares.

SKILL RATING: ● ● ●

MATERIALS

Lily Sugar 'n Cream Super Size Ombres (100% cotton, approx. 138m/150yd per 85g/3oz ball) Aran (worsted) weight yarn:
   3 balls of shade Crown Jewels (A)

Lily Sugar 'n Cream Super Size Solids (100% cotton, approx. 184m/200yd per 113g/4oz ball) Aran (worsted) weight yarn:
   5 balls of shade Ecru (B)

5mm (US size H/8) hook

Yarn needle

FINISHED MEASUREMENTS

Finished blanket is 112cm (44in) square

TENSION (GAUGE)

Each finished square = 19cm (7½in) square.

ABBREVIATIONS

See page 9.

For the blanket

SQUARE (MAKE 25)

Using a 5mm (US size H/8) hook and yarn A, make a magic ring.

Round 1: Ch3 (counts as 1tr), 11tr into the ring, join with a sl st in 3rd of 3-ch. *12 tr.*

Round 2: Ch3 (counts as 1tr), 1tr in same st, 2tr in each st to end, join with a sl st in 3rd of 3-ch. *24 tr.*

Round 3: Ch3 (counts as 1tr), 1tr in same st, 1tr in next st, *2tr in next st, 1tr in next st; rep from * to end, join with a sl st in 3rd of 3-ch. *36 tr.*

SQUARE OFF THE CIRCLE

Change to yarn B.

Round 4: Ch3 (counts as 1tr), 1tr in same st, ch1, 2tr in next st, 1htr in each of next 2 sts, 1dc in each of next 3 sts, 1htr in each of next 2 sts, *2tr in next st, ch1, 2tr in next st, 1htr in each of next 2 sts, 1dc in each of next 3 sts, 1htr in each of next 2 sts; rep from * twice more, join with a sl st in 3rd of 3-ch. *44 sts + four 1-ch sps.*

You might find it quicker to work in a production-line style, first creating all the circles for the centres of the squares, then turning them all into squares before joining them together.

MAKE IT YOURS / Add in circles in solid shades to create a contrast with the variegated yarns.

Using a slip stitch to join the blocks together leaves a neat flush stitch on the surface.

Round 5: Ch3 (counts as 1tr), 1tr in next st, (2tr, ch1, 2tr) in corner sp, *1tr in each st to next corner sp, (2tr, ch1, 2tr) in corner sp; rep from * twice more, 1tr in each st to end, join with a sl st in 3rd of 3-ch. *60 sts + four 1-ch sps.*

Round 6: Ch3 (counts as 1tr), *1tr in each st to next corner sp, (2tr, ch2, 2tr) in corner sp; rep from * 3 more times, 1tr in each st to end, join with a sl st in 3rd of 3-ch. *76 sts + four 1-ch sps.*

Fasten off.

Making up and finishing

Place blocks RS up in five rows of five. Using a 5mm (US size H/8) hook and yarn B, join with sl st through matching sts on each block.

FOR THE BORDER

Round 1: With RS facing, using a 5mm (US size H/8) hook, join yarn A in first st after any corner, ch1, *1dc in each st to next corner, (1dc, ch1, 1dc) in corner; rep from * 3 more times, join with a sl st in first dc.

Rounds 2–4: Change to Yarn B, ch3 (counts as 1tr), *1tr in each st to next corner sp, (2tr, ch2, 2tr) in corner sp; rep from * 3 more times, 1tr in each st to end, join with a sl st in 3rd of 3-ch.

Rounds 5–6: Change to Yarn A, ch1, *1dc in each st to next corner sp, (1dc, ch1, 1dc) in corner sp; rep from * 3 more times, 1dc in each st to end, join with a sl st in first dc.

Fasten off.

Weave in all ends and block as desired to neaten.

MERMAID *Magic*

Transform yourself into a cosy mermaid with this seamed body-shaped blanket, complete with fun tail fins!

SKILL RATING: ● ● ●

MATERIALS

Stylecraft Special XL Super Chunky (100% acrylic, approx. 136m/148yd per 200g/7oz ball) super chunky (super bulky) weight yarn:
  4 balls of shade Sage 3056 (A)
  2 balls of shade Duck Egg 1820 (B)

10mm (US size N/15) and 15mm (US size Q) hooks

FINISHED MEASUREMENTS

Finished blanket is 109cm (43in) long (excluding fin)

TENSION (GAUGE)

6 tr x 3.5 rows = 10cm (4in) square, using 10mm (US size N/15) hook.

ABBREVIATIONS

See page 9.

For the tail

Using a 10mm (US size N/15) hook and yarn A, work a foundation ch of 67 sts.

Row 1: 1tr in 3rd ch from hook, 1tr in each st to end. *65 tr.*

Row 2: Ch3 (counts as 1tr throughout), 1tr in each st to end.

Row 3: Change to yarn B, ch3, 1tr in each st to end.

Row 4: Ch3, 1tr in each st to end.

Rows 5–6: Change to yarn A, ch3, 1tr in each st to end.

Rows 7–8: Change to yarn B, ch3, 1tr in each st to end.

Rows 9–10: Change to yarn A, ch3, 1tr in each st to end.

Row 11: Change to yarn B, ch3, tr2tog, 1tr in each st to last 3 sts, tr2tog, 1tr in last st. *63 tr.*

Row 12: Ch3, 1tr in each st to end.

Row 13: Change to yarn A, ch3, tr2tog, 1tr in each st to last 3 sts, tr2tog, 1tr in last st. *61 tr.*

Row 14: Ch3, 1tr in each st to end.

Row 15: Change to yarn B, ch3, tr2tog, 1tr in each st to last 3 sts, tr2tog, 1tr in last st. *59 tr.*

Row 16: Ch3, 1tr in each st to end.

Row 17: Change to yarn A, ch3, tr2tog, 1tr in each st to last 3 sts, tr2tog, 1tr in last st. *57 tr.*

Row 18: Ch3, 1tr in each st to end.

Row 19: Change to yarn B, ch3, tr2tog, 1tr in each st to last 3 sts, tr2tog, 1tr in last st. *55 tr.*

You can check the length of the blanket as you work by holding it against your body, increasing or decreasing as needed.

Row 20: Ch3, 1tr in each st to end.
Row 21: Change to yarn A, ch3, tr2tog, 1tr in each st to last 3 sts, tr2tog, 1tr in last st. *53 tr.*
Row 22: Ch3, tr2tog, 1tr in each st to last 3 sts, tr2tog, 1tr in last st. *51 tr.*
Row 23: Change to yarn B, ch3, tr2tog, 1tr in each st to last 3 sts, tr2tog, 1tr in last st. *49 tr.*
Row 24: Ch3, tr2tog, 1tr in each st to last 3 sts, tr2tog, 1tr in last st. *47 tr.*
Row 25: Change to yarn A, ch3, tr2tog, 1tr in each st to last 3 sts, tr2tog, 1tr in last st. *45 tr.*
Row 26: Ch3, tr2tog, 1tr in each st to last 3 sts, tr2tog, 1tr in last st. *43 tr.*
Row 27: Change to yarn B, ch3, 1tr in each st to end.
Cont for 13 more rows (or to desired length).
Fasten off.

For the tail fin (make 2)

Using a 15mm (US size Q) hook and yarn A, work a foundation ch of 22 sts.
Row 1: 1tr in 3rd ch from hook, 1tr in each st to end. *20 tr.*
Row 2: Ch3, 1tr in each st to end.
Row 3: Ch3 (counts as 1tr throughout), tr2tog, 1tr in each st to end. *19 tr.*
Row 4: Ch3, 1tr in each st to end.
Row 5: Ch3, tr2tog, 1tr in each st to end. *18 tr.*
Row 6: Ch3, 1tr in each st to end.
Row 7: Ch3, tr2tog twice, 1tr in each st to end. *16 tr.*
Row 8: Ch3, 1tr in each st to end.
Row 9: Ch3, tr2tog twice, 1tr in each st to end. *14 tr.*
Row 10: Ch3, 1tr in each st to end.
Row 11: Ch3, tr2tog twice, 1tr in each st to end. *12 tr.*
Fasten off.
Make second piece to match, don't cut yarn, place with short edges aligned to first piece and join with a sl st through each st.
Fasten off.

Making up and finishing

Fold the outer edges of the tail blanket in towards the centre. Working from the bottom (narrower) end and using the 15mm (US size Q) hook and yarn B, begin joining the centre back seam using sl st. Once the centre back seam is 54cm (21in) long, fasten off.
Place the fin centred in the bottom of blanket – there will be 20cm (8in) excess either side. Using the 15mm (US size Q) hook and yarn B, work with sl st through all 3 layers to close the base of the tail, securing the centre section of the fin as you work.
Fold the two outer corners of the fin (the excess at each side) inwards and sew to secure.
Weave in all ends and block as desired to neaten.

Tip

The seams are worked with slip stitches; leave longer yarn ends that can be used to work these seams.

VINTAGE LACE

Granny Squares

Inspired by vintage china crockery, these lacy granny squares can be joined-as-you-go for a quick and easy finish.

SKILL RATING: ● ● ○

MATERIALS
Schachenmayr Catania (100% cotton, approx. 125m/137yd per 50g/1¾oz ball) 5-ply (sport) weight yarn:
  10 balls of shade Creme 0130 (A)
  5 balls of shade Hellblau 0173 (B)

4mm (US size G/6) hook

Yarn needle

FINISHED MEASUREMENTS
Finished blanket is 114cm (45in) square

TENSION (GAUGE)
Each square measures 10cm (4in) square, using 4mm (US size G/6) hook.

ABBREVIATIONS
See page 9.

SPECIAL ABBREVIATIONS
PS (puff stitch) – *yrh, insert hook into sp, yrh, draw yarn through, keeping yarn loops long; rep from * 5 more times, yrh, draw yarn through all loops on hook, ch1 to close st
Picot – insert hook in ch just below hook, sl st to create small picot

For the blanket

LACE GRANNY SQUARE

Using a 4mm (US size G/6) hook and yarn A, make a magic ring.
Round 1: 12dc into the ring, join with a sl st in first dc. *12 sts.*
Round 2: Ch5 (counts as 1tr + 2ch), *1tr in next dc, ch2; rep from * 10 more times, join with a sl st in 3rd of 5-ch. *12 sts.*
Round 3: *PS in next ch sp, ch2; rep from * to end, join with a sl st in top of first PS. *12 PS.*
Round 4: *1dc in next ch sp, ch3, picot, ch3, 1dc in next ch sp, (1htr, 4tr, ch4, 4tr, 1htr) in next ch sp, to make corner; rep from * 3 more times, join with a sl st in first dc. Fasten off.
Rep to make 84 squares in yarn A and 37 in yarn B, 121 squares in total, joining as you work:

The centre of each square is made with a magic ring; be sure to draw it up fully to close the hole for a neat finish.

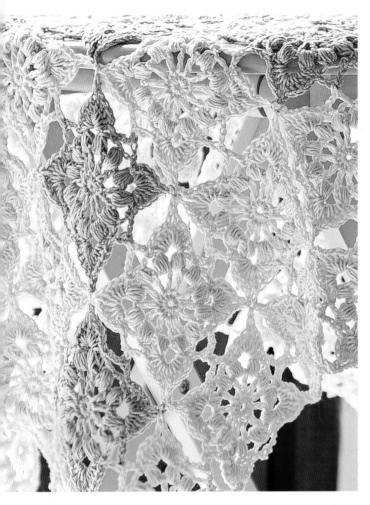

JOIN-AS-YOU-GO

Once one square is complete the square next to it can be joined on in the final round. This is done at each corner and picot point of the joining edge or edges by passing the loop of the stitch that you are making on the current square through the corresponding stitches of the other square, before continuing with the stitch. Continue in this manner, adding on each new square as the round is worked.

SQUARES LAYOUT (11 SQUARES X 11 ROWS)

Row 1: Yarn B x 1, yarn A x 9, yarn B x 1.
Row 2: Yarn A x 1, yarn B x 1, yarn A x 3, yarn B x 1, yarn A x 3, yarn B x 1, yarn A x 1.
Row 3: Yarn A x 2, yarn B x 1, yarn A x 1, yarn B x 1, yarn A x 1, yarn B x 1, yarn A x 1, yarn B x 1, yarn A x 2.
Row 4: Yarn A x 3, yarn B x 1, yarn A x 1, yarn B x 1, yarn A x 1, yarn B x 1, yarn A x 3.
Row 5: Yarn A x 2, yarn B x 1, yarn A x 1, yarn B x 1, yarn A x 1, yarn B x 1, yarn A x 1, yarn B x 1, yarn A x 2.
Row 6: Yarn A x 1, yarn B x 1, yarn A x 1, yarn B x 1, yarn A x 1, yarn B x 1, yarn A x 1, yarn B x 1, yarn A x 1, yarn B x 1, yarn A x 1.
Row 7: Yarn A x 2, yarn B x 1, yarn A x 1, yarn B x 1, yarn A x 1, yarn B x 1, yarn A x 1, yarn B x 1, yarn A x 2.
Row 8: Yarn A x 3, yarn B x 1, yarn A x 1, yarn B x 1, yarn A x 1, yarn B x 1, yarn A x 3.
Row 9: Yarn A x 2, yarn B x 1, yarn A x 1, yarn B x 1, yarn A x 1, yarn B x 1, yarn A x 1, yarn B x 1, yarn A x 2.
Row 10: Yarn A x 1, yarn B x 1, yarn A x 3, yarn B x 1, yarn A x 3, yarn B x 1, yarn A x 1.
Row 11: Yarn B x 1, yarn A x 9, yarn B x 1.

Making up and finishing

Weave in all ends and block as desired to neaten.

These squares are joined-as-you-go, meaning one square is added to the previous on the final round. Working from left to right across the blanket in rows will help you to keep track of your place.

DIAGONAL *Lines*

This blanket is worked from one corner diagonally in rows to the opposite corner, by increasing blocks until the centre row then decreasing to make a neat square.

SKILL RATING: ● ● ●

MATERIALS
Lion Brand Vanna's Choice (100% acrylic, approx. 156m/170yd per 100g/3½oz ball) Aran (worsted) weight yarn:
  2 balls each of shades:
    Silver Blue 105 (A)
    Linen 099 (B)
    Pistachio 169 (C)
  1 ball each of shades:
    Pink 101 (D)
    White 100 (E)

6mm (US size J/10) hook

Yarn needle

FINISHED MEASUREMENTS
Finished blanket is 107cm (42in) square

TENSION (GAUGE)
Four 3-tr blocks x 4.5 rows = 10cm (4in) in stitch patt, using 6mm (US size J/10) hook.

ABBREVIATIONS
See page 9.

For the blanket

Using a 6mm (US size J/10) hook and yarn A, work a foundation ch of 6 sts.
Row 1: 1tr in 4th ch from hook, 1tr in each of next 2 sts. *One 3-tr block.*
Row 2: Turn work, ch6, 1tr in 4th ch from hook, 1tr in each of next 2 sts, sl st in ch sp on block from previous row, ch3 (counts as 1tr), 3tr in same sp. *Two 3-tr blocks.*
Row 3: Turn work, ch6, 1tr in 4th ch from hook, 1tr in each of next 2 sts, sl st in ch sp on first block from previous row, ch3 (counts as 1tr), 3tr in same sp, sl st in ch sp on 2nd block from previous row, ch3 (counts as 1tr), 3tr in same sp. *Three 3-tr blocks.*
Cont in patt as set for a further 20 rows, 23 rows in total. *Twenty-three 3-tr blocks.*
Cont in patt as set, working foll colour sequence:
Yarn B for 4 rows. *Twenty-seven 3-tr blocks.*
Yarn C for 4 rows. *Thirty-one 3-tr blocks.*
Yarn B for 4 rows. *Thirty-five 3-tr blocks.*
Yarn C for 4 rows. *Thirty-nine 3-tr blocks.*
Yarn D for 3 rows. *Forty-two 3-tr blocks.*

The stitches form blocks, making it easy to keep track of where you are, adding or removing one block from each end of the row.

Once you begin decreasing you will be omitting the chain at the start of the row and this reduces the number of blocks per row.

BEGIN DECREASING

Cont with yarn D, turn work, sl st in 3 sts on first block in row, *sl st in ch sp on next block from previous row, ch3 (counts as 1tr), 3tr in same sp; rep from * to last block, sl st in ch sp on last block, turn for next row.
This sets patt for dec, cont in dec patt as set in foll colour sequence until one block remains:
Yarn D for 1 row. *Forty 3-tr blocks.*
Yarn C for 4 rows. *Thirty-six 3-tr blocks.*
Yarn B for 4 rows. *Thirty-two 3-tr blocks.*
Yarn C for 4 rows. *Twenty-eight 3-tr blocks.*
Yarn B for 4 rows. *Twenty-four 3-tr blocks.*
Yarn A for 23 rows. *One 3-tr block.*
Fasten off.

FOR THE BORDER

Round 1: With RS facing, using a 6mm (US size J/10) hook, join yarn E in first st after any corner, ch1, *1dc in each st to next corner, (1dc, ch1, 1dc) in corner; rep from * 3 more times, join with a sl st in first dc.
Round 2: Ch3 (counts as tr), *1tr in each st to next corner sp, (1tr, ch2, 1tr) in corner sp; rep from * 3 more times, join with a sl st in 3rd of 3-ch.
Round 3: Ch1, *1dc in each st to next corner sp, (1dc, ch1, 1dc) in corner sp; rep from * 3 more times, join with a sl st in first dc.
Fasten off.

Making up and finishing

Weave in all ends and block as desired to neaten.

MAKE IT YOURS / You can increase the size by working more rows before beginning to decrease – remember to increase the yarn amounts accordingly.

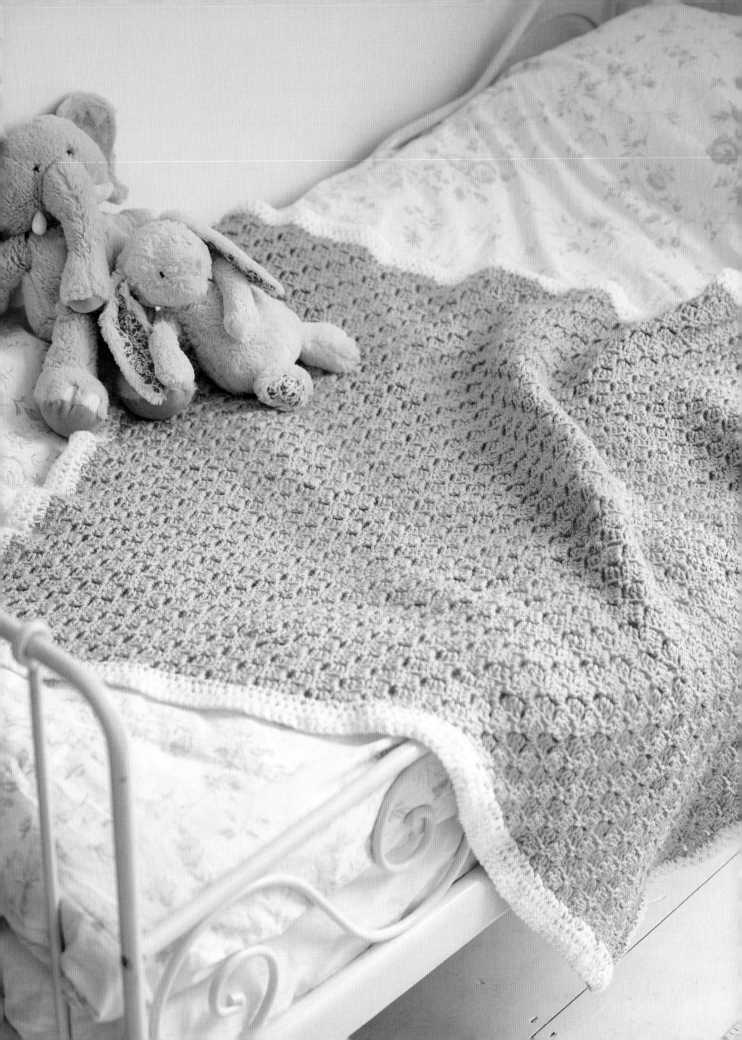

THE SEA

At Night

The half-square triangle is a simple yet extremely versatile design – make this cosy blanket as shown, or create your own striking geometric patterns.

SKILL RATING: ● ● ●

MATERIALS

Rowan Handknit Cotton DK (100% cotton, approx. 85m/93yd per 50g/1¾oz ball) DK (light worsted) weight yarn:

5 balls each of shades:
  Linen 205 (A)
  Sea Foam 352 (B)
  Slate 347 (C)

4.5mm (US size 7) hook

Yarn needle

FINISHED MEASUREMENTS

Finished blanket is 107cm (42in) square

TENSION (GAUGE)

Each square measures 15cm (6in), using 4.5mm (US size 7) hook.

ABBREVIATIONS

See page 9.

For the blanket

HALF-SQUARE GRANNY SQUARES (MAKE 6 IN EACH COLOUR COMBINATION, 18 TOTAL)

Using a 4.5mm (US size 7) hook and yarn A, make a magic ring.

Round 1: Ch3 (counts as 1tr throughout), 2tr into ring, ch2, 3tr into the ring, ch1, change to yarn B (don't cut yarn A), ch1, [3tr into the ring, ch2] twice, sl st in 3rd of 3-ch, turn, sl st in ch sp.

Round 2: Cont in yarn B, ch3, 1tr in same sp, 1tr in each of next 3 sts, (2tr, 2ch, 2tr) in ch sp, 1tr in each of next 3 sts, 2tr in ch sp, ch1, pick up yarn A (don't cut yarn B), ch1, 2tr in same ch sp, 1tr in each of next 3 sts, (2tr, 2ch, 2tr) in ch sp, 1tr in each of next 3 sts, 2tr in ch sp, ch2, join with a sl s in 3rd of 3-ch, turn, sl st in ch sp.

Round 3: Cont in yarn A, ch3, 1tr in same sp, 1tr in each of next 7 sts, (2tr, 2ch, 2tr) in ch sp, 1tr in each of next 7 sts, 2tr in ch sp, 1ch, pick up yarn B (don't cut yarn A), ch1, 2tr in same ch sp, 1tr in each of next 7 sts, (2tr, 2ch, 2tr) in ch sp, 1tr in each of next 7 sts, 2tr in ch sp, 2ch, join with a sl st in 3rd of 3-ch, turn, sl st in ch sp.

Round 4: Cont in yarn B, ch3, 1tr in same sp, 1tr in each of next 11 sts, (2tr, 2ch, 2tr) in ch sp, 1tr in each of next 11 sts, 2tr in ch sp, ch1, pick up yarn A (don't cut yarn B), ch1, 2tr in same ch sp, 1tr in each of next 11 sts, (2tr, 2ch, 2tr) in ch sp, 1tr in each of next 11 sts, 2tr in ch sp, 2ch, join with a sl st in 3rd of 3-ch, turn, sl st in ch sp.

Round 5: Cont in yarn A, ch3, 1tr in same sp, 1tr in each of next 15 sts, (2tr, 2ch, 2tr) in ch-sp, 1tr in each of next 15 sts, 2tr in ch sp, ch1, pick up to yarn B (fasten off yarn A), ch1, 2tr in ch sp, 1tr in each of next 15 sts, (2tr, 2ch, 2tr) in ch sp, 1tr in each of next 15 sts, 2tr in ch sp, 2ch, join with a sl st in 3rd of 3-ch.
Fasten off.

These squares are flipped so as not to carry the yarn around the whole square. You will be able to tell what direction to work in by the position of the alternate colour yarn.

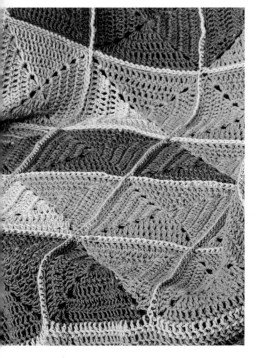

SOLID GRANNY SQUARE (MAKE 6 IN EACH COLOUR, 18 TOTAL)

Using a 4.5mm (US size 7) hook and yarn A, make a magic ring.

Round 1: Ch3 (counts as 1tr throughout), 2tr into the ring, *(ch2, 3tr) into the ring; rep from * twice more, ch2, join with a sl st in 3rd of 3-ch.

Round 2: Change to yarn B, ch3, 1tr in each of next 2 sts, (2tr, 2ch, 2tr) in ch sp, *1tr in each of next 3 sts, (2tr, 2ch, 2tr) in ch sp; rep from * twice more, join with a sl st in 3rd of 3-ch.

Round 3: Change to yarn C, ch3, 1tr in each of next 4 sts, (2tr, 2ch, 2tr) in ch sp, *1tr in each of next 7 sts, (2tr, 2ch, 2tr) in ch sp; rep from * twice more, 1tr in each of next 2 sts, join with a sl st in 3rd of 3-ch.

Round 4: Change to yarn D, ch3, 1tr in each of next 6 sts, (2tr, 2ch, 2tr) in ch sp, *1tr in each of next 11 sts, (2tr, 2ch, 2tr) in ch sp; rep from * twice more, 1tr in each of next 4 sts, join with a sl st in 3rd of 3-ch.

Round 5: Change to yarn E, ch3, 1tr in each of next 8 sts, (2tr, 2ch, 2tr) in ch sp, *1tr in each of next 15 sts, (2tr, 2ch, 2tr) in ch sp; rep from * twice more, 1tr in each of next 6 sts, join with a sl st in 3rd of 3-ch.

Fasten off.

Making up and finishing

Arrange the squares in your desired pattern in six rows of eight blocks. Using a 4.5mm (US size 7) hook and yarn A, join the squares together with 1dc in each st through both layers, working through the back loops only.

FOR THE BORDER

Round 1: With RS facing, using a 4.5mm (US size 7) hook, join yarn A in first st after any corner, ch3 (counts as 1tr), *1tr in each st to next corner, (1tr, ch1, 1tr) in corner; rep from * 3 more times, join with a sl st in 3rd of 3-ch.

Round 2: Change to yarn B, ch3, *1tr in each st to next corner sp, (1tr, ch1, 1tr) in corner sp; rep from * 3 more times, join with a sl st in 3rd of 3-ch.

Round 3: Change to yarn C, ch3, *1tr in each st to next corner sp, (1tr, ch1, 1tr) in corner sp; rep from * 3 more times, join with a sl st in 3rd of 3-ch.

Fasten off.

Weave in all ends and block as desired to neaten.

Try to maintain an even tension throughout to ensure that the half-triangle squares are the same size as the solid squares.

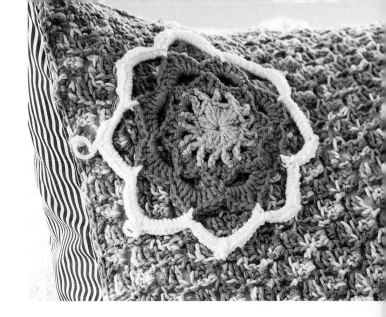

MANDALA *Meditation*

Create a retro-inspired design by teaming a mandala with
a corner-to-corner background panel.

SKILL RATING: ● ● ●

MATERIALS

Berroco Comfort (50% nylon, 50% acrylic, approx.
193m/210yd per 100g/3½oz ball) Aran (worsted)
weight yarn:
  1 ball each of shades:
  Galaxy Mix 9808 (A)
  Goldenrod 9743 (B)
  Persimmon 9783 (C)
  Chalk 9700 (D)

5mm (US size H/8) hook

Yarn needle

63cm (25in) square cushion pad

Cushion cover or fabric to create backing

FINISHED MEASUREMENTS

Finished cushion is 63cm (25in) square

TENSION (GAUGE)

Five 3-tr blocks x 5 rows = 10cm (4in) in stitch patt,
using 5mm (US size H/8) hook.
12 tr x 7 rows = 10cm (4in) in tr, using 5mm (US
size H/8) hook.

ABBREVIATIONS

See page 9.

For the cushion

BACKGROUND PANEL

Using a 5mm (US size H/8) hook and yarn A, work a foundation
ch of 6 sts.
Row 1: 1tr in 4th ch from hook, 1tr in each of next 2 sts. *One
3-tr block*.
Row 2: Turn work, ch6, 1tr in 4th ch from hook, 1tr in each of
next 2 sts, sl st in ch sp on block from previous row, ch3 (counts
as 1tr), 3tr in same sp. *Two 3-tr blocks*.
Row 3: Turn work, ch6, 1tr in 4th ch from hook, 1tr in each of
next 2 sts, sl st in ch sp on first block from previous row, ch3
(counts as 1tr), 3tr in same sp, sl st in ch sp on 2nd block from
previous row, ch3 (counts as 1tr), 3tr in same sp. *Three 3-tr
blocks*.
Cont in patt as set for a further 26 rows, 29 rows in total.
Twenty-nine 3-tr blocks.

BEGIN DECREASING

Turn work, sl st in 3 sts on first block in row, *sl st in ch sp on
next block from previous row, ch3 (counts as 1tr), 3tr in same sp;
rep from * to last block, sl st in ch sp on last block, turn for
next row.
This sets patt for dec, cont in dec patt as set until one
block remains.
Fasten off.

For the mandala

Using a 5mm (US size H/8) hook and yarn B, work a foundation ch of 8 sts, sl st to join into a ring.

Round 1: Ch3 (counts as 1tr throughout), 23tr into ring, join with a sl st in 3rd of 3-ch. *24 sts.*

Round 2: Ch5 (counts as 1tr and 2ch), 1tr in same place as sl st, ch1, *miss next 2tr, (1tr, 2ch, 1tr) in next tr, ch1; rep from * to end, join with a sl st in 3rd of 5-ch. *16 sts + eight 2-ch sps + eight 1-ch sps.*

Round 3: Change to yarn C, sl st in first 2-ch sp, ch3, (1tr, 2ch, 2tr) in same sp, *1dc in next 1-ch sp, (2tr, 2ch, 2tr) in next 2-ch sp; rep from * to end, join with a sl st in 3rd of 3-ch. *40 sts + eight 2-ch sps.*

Round 4: Sl st in first tr and 2-ch sp, 1dc in same sp, ch6, *1dc in next 2-ch sp, ch6; rep from * to end, join with a sl st in first dc. *8 dc + eight 6-ch sps.*

Round 5: Sl st in 6-ch sp, ch3, (3tr, ch2, 4tr) in same sp, *(1dc, 4tr, ch2, 4tr) in next 6-ch sp; rep from * to end, join with a sl st in 3rd of 3-ch. *64 tr + 8 dc + eight 2-ch sps.*

Round 6: Change to yarn D, sl st in next 3 tr and 2-ch sp, 1dc in same sp, ch10, *1dc in next 2-ch sp, ch10; rep from * to end, join with a sl st in first dc. *8 dc + eight 10-ch sps.*

Round 7: *(10dc, ch2, 10dc) in next 10-ch sp; rep from * to end, join with a sl st in first dc. *160 dc + eight 2-ch sps.*

Fasten off.

Making up and finishing

Weave in all ends and block as desired to neaten.
Place panel onto front of fabric cushion cover and stitch to secure.

To create your own fabric backing, cut two pieces of fabric to 45 x 67.5cm (18 x 27in). Fold 2.5cm (1in) to the WS around each side, press and sew in place. Place the two pieces together, both with RS facing up, to create a 62.5cm (25in) square panel – the pieces will overlap in the centre to allow the cushion pad to be inserted. With WS together, place the assembled fabric piece onto the crochet panel and sew around the outer edges.

 The crochet mandala only used small amounts of yarn – if using yarn from your stash, pick yarns with a similar weight.

MAKE IT YOURS / If you prefer to make this cushion cover removable, simply leave one side unsealed and add a series of button loops along one edge and buttons on the other.

SIMPLE *Stripes*

Keep it minimal with neutral tones and simple stitches to create this soft and sumptuous cushion. The order of the stripes is reversed on the back of the cushion.

SKILL RATING: ● ● ●

MATERIALS
Stylecraft Weekender Super Chunky (100% acrylic, approx. 100m/109yd per 100g/3½oz ball) super chunky (super bulky) weight yarn:
  3 balls each of shades:
    Cream 3677 (A)
    Clay 3678 (B)

9mm (US size M/13) hook

Yarn needle

66cm (26in) square cushion pad

FINISHED MEASUREMENTS
Finished cushion is 67cm (26½in) square

TENSION (GAUGE)
6 tr x 4.5 rows = 10cm (4in) square, using 9mm (US size M/13) hook.

ABBREVIATIONS
See page 9.

For the cushion

FRONT

Using a 9mm (US size M/13) hook and yarn A, work a foundation ch of 51 sts.
Row 1: 1dc in 2nd ch from hook, 1dc in each st to end. *50 sts.*
Rows 2–5: Ch3 (counts as 1tr), 1tr in each st to end.
Row 6: Ch1, 1dc in each st to end.
Row 7: Change to yarn B, ch1, 1dc in each st to end.
Rows 2 to 7 form patt. Cont in patt as set, changing colour every 6 rows until 5 colour blocks have been worked in total.
Fasten off.

BACK

Using a 9mm (US size M/13) hook and yarn B, make a foundation ch of 51 sts.
Row 1: 1dc in 2nd ch from hook, 1dc in each st to end. *50 sts.*
Rows 2–5: Ch3 (counts as 1tr), 1tr in each st to end.
Row 6: Ch1, 1dc in each st to end.
Row 7: Change to yarn A, ch1, 1dc in each st to end.
Rows 2 to 7 form patt. Cont in patt as set, changing colour every 6 rows until 5 colour blocks have been worked.
Fasten off.

Making up and finishing

Weave in all ends.
Place front and back panels WS together, with cushion pad between them.
Round 1: Using a 9mm (US size M/13) hook, join yarn B in first st after any corner, *working through both layers, 1dc in each st to next corner, (1dc, ch2, 1dc) in corner; rep from * 3 more times, join with a sl st in first dc.
Fasten off.

Tips

Chunkier yarns sometimes don't fit through the eye of a yarn needle, but you can use a smaller crochet hook to help weave the ends in.

If you prefer to make the front and back of this cushion matching, simply increase the yarn quantities of one shade to ensure that you have enough yarn.

BERMUDA *Triangles*

Crocheted triangles tessellate neatly, to create a striking geometric-design cushion panel worked in cool tonal shades.

SKILL RATING: ● ● �ौ

MATERIALS

Brown Sheep Lamb's Pride Worsted (85% wool, 15% mohair, approx. 173m/190yd per 113g/4oz ball) Aran (worsted) weight yarn:
  1 ball each of shades:
    Blue Flannel M82 (A)
    Oatmeal M115 (B)
    Seafoam M16 (C)
    Turquoise Depths M187 (D)

5.5mm (US size I/9) hook

Yarn needle

63cm (25in) square cushion pad

Cushion cover or fabric to create backing

FINISHED MEASUREMENTS

Finished cushion is 64cm (25½in) square

TENSION (GAUGE)

10 sts x 6 rows = 10cm (4in) square, using 5.5mm (US size I/9) hook.

ABBREVIATIONS

See page 9.

For the panel

TRIANGLES (MAKE 24 IN TOTAL, USING MIX OF YARN SHADES)

Using a 5.5mm (US size I/9) hook and yarn A, work a foundation ch of 16 sts.
Row 1: 1tr in 4th ch from hook (missed 3-ch counts as 1tr), 1tr in each st to end. *14 tr.*
Row 2: Ch3 (counts as 1tr), 1tr in each st to end.
Row 3: Ch3 (counts as 1tr), miss st at base of ch and next st, 1tr in each st to last 2 sts, miss next st, 1tr in 3rd of 3-ch. *12 sts.*
Row 4: Ch3 (counts as 1tr), 1tr in each st to end.
Row 5: Ch3 (counts as 1tr), miss st at base of ch and next st, 1tr in each st to last 2 sts, miss next st, 1 tr in 3rd of 3-ch. *10 sts.*

Leave long yarn ends at the beginning and end of each piece to be used for joining the pieces together.

Row 6: Ch3 (counts as 1tr), 1tr in each st to end.
Cont in patt as set, missing 1 st at each end of every other
row, until 2 sts rem.
Fasten off.

HALF TRIANGLE (MAKE 6 IN TOTAL, USING MIX OF YARN
SHADES)

Using a 5.5mm (US size I/9) hook and yarn A, work a
foundation ch of 10 sts.
Row 1: 1tr in 4th ch from hook (missed 3-ch counts as
1tr), 1tr in each ch to end. *8 sts.*
Row 2: Ch3 (counts as 1tr), 1tr in each st to last 2 sts,
miss next st, 1tr in 3rd of 3-ch. *7 sts.*
Row 3: Ch3 (counts as 1tr), 1tr in each st to end.
Cont in patt as set until 2 sts rem.
Fasten off.

Making up and finishing

Place triangles interlocking in three rows of eight, then
add three half-triangles at each side to create a square.
Use yarn ends to join triangles together with whip stitch.
Weave in all ends.
Place panel onto front of fabric cushion cover and stitch
to secure.

To create your own fabric backing, cut two pieces of fabric
to 45 x 67.5cm (18 x 27in). Fold 2.5cm (1in) to the WS
around each side, press and sew in place. Place the two
pieces together, both with RS facing up, to create a
62.5cm (25in) square panel – the pieces will overlap in the
centre to allow the cushion pad to be inserted. With WS
together, place the assembled fabric piece onto the
crochet panel and sew around the outer edges.

MAKE IT YOURS / Make a multi-coloured design by using up same-weight yarns
from your stash.

TECHNIQUES

In this section, we explain how to master the simple crochet and finishing techniques that you need to make the projects in this book.

Holding the hook

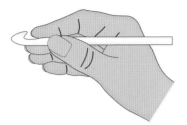

Pick up your hook as though you are picking up a pen or pencil. Keeping the hook held loosely between your fingers and thumb, turn your hand so that the palm is facing up and the hook is balanced in your hand and resting in the space between your index finger and your thumb.

You can also hold the hook like a knife – this may be easier if you are working with a large hook or with chunky yarn. Choose the method that you find most comfortable.

Holding the yarn

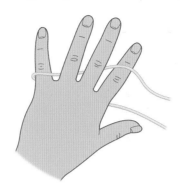

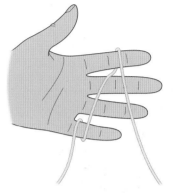

1 Pick up the yarn with your little finger in the opposite hand to your hook, with your palm facing upward and with the short end in front. Turn your hand to face downward, with the yarn on top of your index finger and under the other two fingers and wrapped right around the little finger, as shown above.

2 Turn your hand to face you, ready to hold the work in your middle finger and thumb. Keeping your index finger only at a slight curve, hold the work or the slip knot using the same hand, between your middle finger and your thumb and just below the crochet hook and loop/s on the hook.

Making a slip knot

The simplest way is to make a circle with the yarn, so that the loop is facing downward.

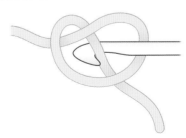

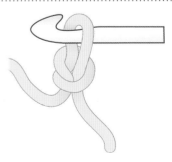

1 In one hand hold the circle at the top where the yarn crosses, and let the tail drop down at the back so that it falls across the centre of the loop. With your free hand or the tip of a crochet hook, pull a loop through the circle.

2 Put the hook into the loop and pull gently so that it forms a loose loop on the hook.

Yarn round hook (yrh)

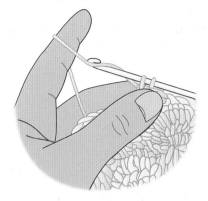

To create a stitch, catch the yarn from behind with the hook pointing upward. As you gently pull the yarn through the loop on the hook, turn the hook so it faces downward and slide the yarn through the loop. The loop on the hook should be kept loose enough for the hook to slide through easily.

Magic ring

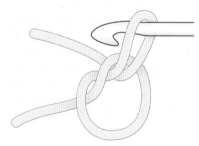

This is a useful starting technique if you do not want a visible hole in the centre of your round. Loop the yarn around your finger, insert the hook through the ring, yarn round hook, and pull through the ring to make the first chain. Work the number of stitches required into the ring and then pull the end to tighten the centre ring and close the hole.

Chain (ch)

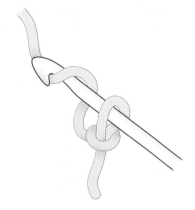

1 Using the hook, wrap the yarn round the hook ready to pull it through the loop on the hook.

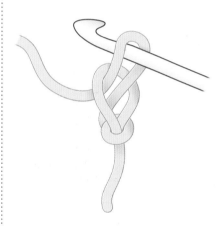

2 Pull through, creating a new loop on the hook. Continue in this way to create a chain of the required length.

Chain ring

If you are crocheting a round shape, one way of starting off is by crocheting a number of chains following the instructions in your pattern, and then joining them into a circle.

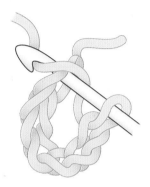

1 To join the chain into a circle, insert the crochet hook into the first chain that you made (not into the slip knot), yarn round hook.

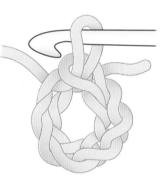

2 Pull the yarn through the chain and through the loop on your hook at the same time, thereby creating a slip stitch and forming a circle. You now have a chain ring ready to work stitches into as instructed in the pattern.

Chain space (ch sp)

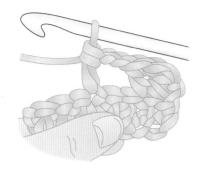

1 A chain space is the space that has been made under a chain in the previous round or row, and falls in between other stitches.

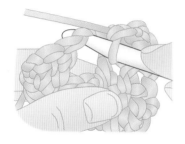

2 Stitches into a chain space are made directly into the hole created under the chain and not into the chain stitches themselves.

Slip stitch (sl st)

A slip stitch doesn't create any height and is often used as the last stitch to create a smooth and even round or row.

1 To make a slip stitch: first put the hook through the work, yarn round hook.

2 Pull the yarn through both the work and through the loop on the hook at the same time, so you will have 1 loop on the hook.

Making rounds

When working in rounds the work is not turned, so you are always working from one side. Depending on the pattern you are working, a 'round' can be square. Start each round by making one or more chains to create the height you need for the stitch you are working:
Double crochet = 1 chain
Half treble crochet = 2 chains
Treble crochet = 3 chains
Double treble = 4 chains
Work the required stitches to complete the round. At the end of the round, slip stitch into the top of the chain to close the round.

If you work in a spiral you do not need a turning chain. After completing the base ring, place a stitch marker in the first stitch and then continue to crochet around. When you have made a round and reached the point where the stitch marker is, work this stitch, take out the stitch marker from the previous round and put it back into the first stitch of the new round. A safety pin or piece of yarn in a contrasting colour makes a good stitch marker.

Making rows

When making straight rows you turn the work at the end of each row and make a turning chain to create the height you need for the stitch you are working with, as for making rounds.
Double crochet = 1 chain
Half treble crochet = 2 chains
Treble crochet = 3 chains
Double treble = 4 chains

Working into top of stitch

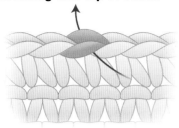

Unless otherwise directed, always insert the hook under both of the two loops on top of the stitch – this is the standard technique.

Working into front loop of stitch (FLO)

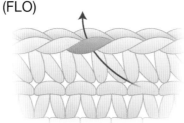

To work into the front loop of a stitch, pick up the front loop from underneath at the front of the work.

Working into back loop of stitch (BLO)

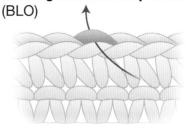

To work into the back loop of the stitch, insert the hook between the front and the back loop, picking up the back loop from the front of the work.

How to measure a tension (gauge) square

Using the hook and the yarn recommended in the pattern, make a number of chains to measure approximately 15cm (6in). Working in the stitch pattern given for the tension measurements, work enough rows to form a square. Fasten off.

Take a ruler, place it horizontally across the square, and using pins, mark a 10cm (4in) area. Repeat vertically to form a 10cm (4in) square on the fabric. Count the number of stitches across, and the number of rows within the square, and compare against the tension given in the pattern.

If your numbers match the pattern then use this size hook and yarn for your project. If you have more stitches, then your tension is tighter than recommended and you need to use a larger hook. If you have fewer stitches, then your tension is looser and you will need a smaller hook.

Make tension squares using different size hooks until you have matched the tension in the pattern, and use this hook to make the project.

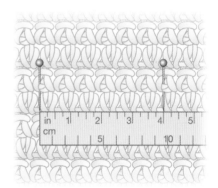

Double crochet (dc)

1 Insert the hook into your work, yarn round hook and pull the yarn through the work only. You will then have 2 loops on the hook.

2 Yarn round hook again and pull through the two loops on the hook. You will then have 1 loop on the hook.

Half treble crochet (htr)

1 Before inserting the hook into the work, wrap the yarn round the hook and put the hook through the work with the yarn wrapped around.

2 Yarn round hook again and pull through the first loop on the hook. You now have 3 loops on the hook.

3 Yarn round hook and pull the yarn through all 3 loops. You will be left with 1 loop on the hook.

Treble crochet (tr)

1 Before inserting the hook into the work, wrap the yarn round the hook. Put the hook through the work with the yarn wrapped around, yarn round hook again and pull through the first loop on the hook. You now have 3 loops on the hook.

2 Yarn round hook again, pull the yarn through the first 2 loops on the hook. You now have 2 loops on the hook.

3 Pull the yarn through 2 loops again. You will be left with 1 loop on the hook.

Double treble (dtr)

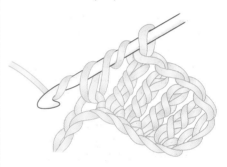

Yarn round hook twice, insert hook into the stitch, yarn round hook, pull a loop through (4 loops on hook), yarn round hook, pull the yarn through 2 stitches (3 loops on hook), yarn round hook, pull a loop through the next 2 stitches (2 loops on hook), yarn round hook, pull a loop through the last 2 stitches.

Puff stitch (PS)

A puff stitch is a padded stitch worked by creating several loops on the hook before completing the stitch. The basic principle is always the same, but you can repeat steps 1 and 2 fewer times to make a smaller puff. Sometimes a chain is worked at the end to secure the puff stitch.

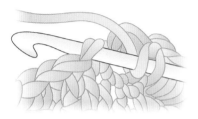

1 Yarn round hook, and insert the hook into the next stitch or space.

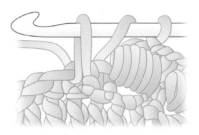

2 Yarn round hook again and draw through, keeping the loops of yarn long.

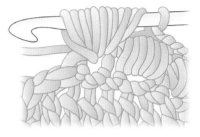

3 Repeat steps 1 and 2 five more times, keeping the loops long each time. There will be 13 loops on the hook.

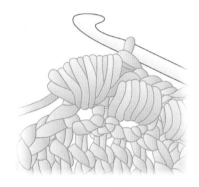

4 Yarn round hook and draw through all the loops on the hook.

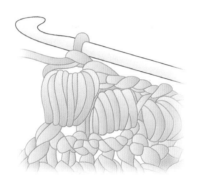

5 Yarn round hook, and draw through the single loop on the hook to make a chain and secure the puff stitch.

Bobble

A bobble is similar to a puff stitch, but you work a complete stitch at the start and then continue taking the yarn round the hook and drawing through the stitch to make the bobble as large as you like. Sometimes a chain is worked at the end to secure the bobble.

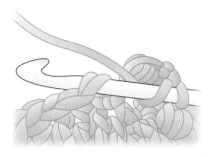

1 Yarn round the hook and insert the hook into the next stitch.

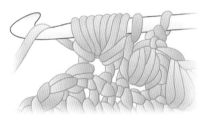

2 Yarn round hook and draw through the stitch.

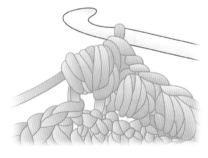

3 Yarn round hook, and draw through the first two loops on the hook.

4 Yarn round the hook, insert the hook into the same stitch, yarn round hook and draw through the stitch.

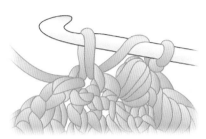

5 Repeat step 4 three more times, keeping the loops long. There will be 10 loops on the hook. Wrap the yarn around the hook.

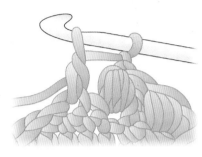

6 Then draw the yarn through all the loops on the hook to complete the bobble stitch.

7 (Optional): yarn round hook, and draw the yarn through the single loop on the hook to make a chain and secure the bobble.

Clusters

Clusters are groups of stitches, with each stitch only partly worked and then all joined at the end to form one stitch that creates a particular pattern and shape. They are most effective when made using a longer stitch such as a treble.

THREE-TREBLE CLUSTER (3trcl)

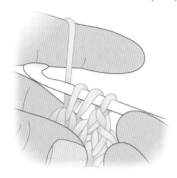

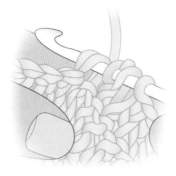

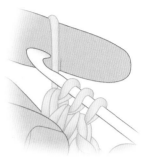

1 Yarn round hook, insert the hook in the stitch (or space). Yarn round hook, draw the yarn through the work (3 loops on the hook).

2 Yarn round hook, draw the yarn through 2 loops on the hook (2 loops on the hook). Yarn round hook, insert the hook in the same stitch (or space).

3 Yarn round hook, draw the yarn through the work (4 loops on the hook). Yarn round hook, draw the yarn through 2 loops on the hook (3 loops on the hook).

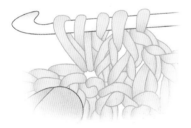

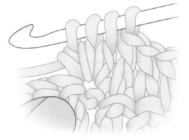

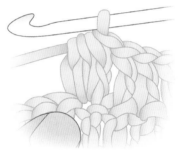

4 Yarn round hook, insert the hook in the same stitch (or space), yarn round hook, draw the yarn through the work (5 loops on the hook).

5 Yarn round hook, draw the yarn through 2 loops on the hook (4 loops on the hook).

6 Yarn round hook, draw the yarn through all 4 loops on the hook (1 loop on the hook).

FOUR-TREBLE CLUSTER (4trcl)

Work steps 1 to 4 and then repeat steps 4 and 5 again (5 loops on the hook). Yarn round hook, draw the yarn through all 5 loops on the hook (1 loop on the hook).

Increasing

Make two or three stitches into one stitch or space from the previous row. The illustration shows a treble crochet increase being made.

Decreasing

You can decrease by either missing the next stitch and continuing to crochet, or by crocheting two or more stitches together. The basic technique for crocheting stitches together is the same, no matter which stitch you are using. The following examples show dc2tog and tr2tog.

DOUBLE CROCHET TWO STITCHES TOGETHER (dc2tog)

1 Insert the hook into your work, yarn round hook and pull the yarn through the work (2 loops on hook). Insert the hook in next stitch, yarn round hook and pull the yarn through.

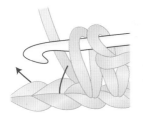

2 Yarn round hook again and pull through all 3 loops on the hook. You will then have 1 loop on the hook.

TREBLE CROCHET TWO STITCHES TOGETHER (tr2tog)

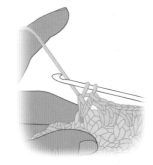

1 Yarn round hook, insert the hook into the next space, yarn round hook, pull the yarn through the work (3 loops on hook).

2 Yarn round hook, pull the yarn through 2 loops on the hook (2 loops on hook).

3 Yarn round hook, insert the hook into the next space.

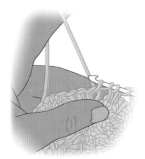

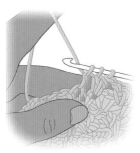

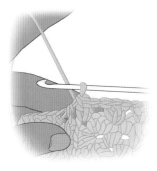

4 Yarn round hook, pull the yarn through the work (4 loops on hook).

5 Yarn round hook, pull the yarn through 2 loops on the hook (3 loops on hook).

6 Yarn round hook, pull the yarn through all 3 loops on the hook (1 loop on hook).

TREBLE CROCHET THREE STITCHES TOGETHER (tr3tog)
This stitch decreases three treble stitches into one.

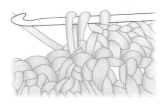 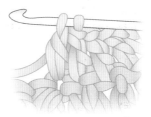 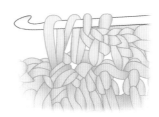 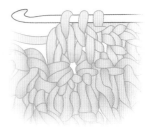

1 Yarn round hook, insert the hook in the next stitch, yarn round hook, draw up a loop (3 loops on hook).

2 Yarn round hook, and draw through the first 2 loops on the hook (2 loops on hook).

3 Yarn round hook, insert the hook in the next stitch, yarn round hook, draw up a loop (4 loops on hook).

4 Yarn round hook, and draw through the first 2 loops on the hook (3 loops on hook).

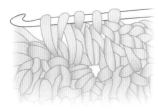 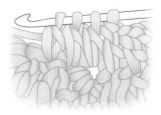 

5 Yarn round hook, insert the hook in the next stitch, yarn round hook, draw up a loop (5 loops on hook).

6 Yarn round hook, and draw through the first 2 loops on the hook (4 loops on hook).

7 Yarn round hook, and draw through all 4 loops on the hook (1 loop on hook).

Joining yarn at the end of a row or round
You can use this technique when changing colour, or when joining in a new ball of yarn as one runs out.

1 Keep the loop of the old yarn on the hook. Drop the tail and catch a loop of the strand of the new yarn with the crochet hook.

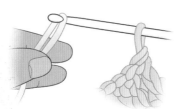

2 Draw the new yarn through the loop on the hook, keeping the old loop drawn tight and continue as instructed in the pattern.

Joining in new yarn after fastening off

1 Fasten off the old colour (see page 125). Make a slip knot with the new colour (see page 115). Insert the hook into the stitch at the beginning of the next row, then through the slip knot.

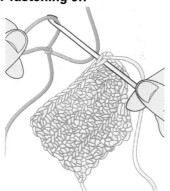

2 Draw the loop of the slip knot through to the front of the work. Carry on working using the new colour, following the instructions in the pattern.

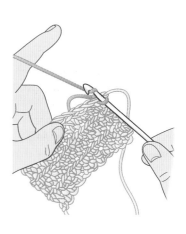

Joining yarn in the middle of a row or round

For a neat colour join in the middle of a row or round, use these methods.

JOINING A NEW COLOUR INTO DOUBLE CROCHET

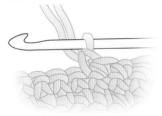 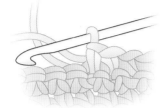

1 Make a double crochet stitch (see page 118), but do not draw the final loop through, so there are 2 loops on the hook. Drop the old yarn, catch the new yarn with the hook and draw it through both loops to complete the stitch and join in the new colour at the same time.

2 Continue to crochet with the new yarn. Cut the old yarn leaving a 15cm (6in) tail and weave the tail in (see right) after working a row, or once the work is complete.

JOINING A NEW COLOUR INTO TREBLE CROCHET

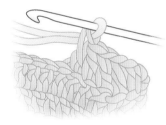 

1 Make a treble crochet stitch (see page 119), but do not draw the final loop through, so there are 2 loops on the hook. Drop the old yarn, catch the new yarn with the hook and draw it through both loops to complete the stitch and join in the new colour at the same time.

2 Continue to crochet with the new yarn. Cut the old yarn leaving a 15cm (6in) tail and weave the tail in (see right) after working a row, or once the work is complete.

Enclosing a yarn tail

You may find that the yarn tail gets in the way as you work; you can enclose this into the stitches as you go by placing the tail at the back as you wrap the yarn. This also saves having to sew this tail end in later.

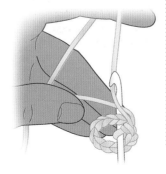

Fastening off

When you have finished crocheting, you need to fasten off the stitches to stop all your work unravelling.

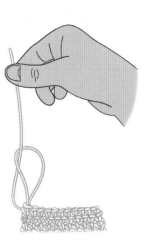

1 Draw up the final loop of the last stitch to make it bigger. Cut the yarn, leaving a tail of approx. 10cm (4in) – unless a longer end is needed for sewing up. Pull the tail all the way through the loop and pull the loop up tightly.

Weaving in yarn ends

It is important to weave in the tail ends of the yarn so that they are secure and your crochet won't unravel. Thread a tapestry needle with the tail end of yarn. On the wrong side, take the needle through the crochet one stitch down on the edge, then take it through the stitches, working in a gentle zig-zag. Work through four or five stitches then return in the opposite direction. Remove the needle, pull the crochet gently to stretch it, and trim the end.

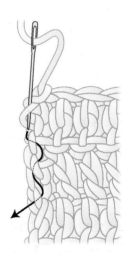

Sewing up

Sewing up crochet fabric can be done in many ways, but using a whip stitch is the easiest. However, you will be able to see the stitches clearly, so use a matching yarn. Lay the two pieces to be joined next to each other with right sides facing upward. Secure the yarn to one piece. Insert the needle into the front of one piece of fabric, then up from the back of the adjoining fabric. Repeat along the seam.

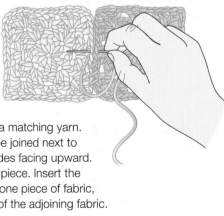
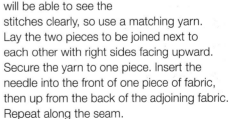

Making a double crochet seam

With a double crochet seam you join two pieces together using a crochet hook and working a double crochet stitch through both pieces, instead of sewing them together with a tail of yarn and a yarn sewing needle. This makes a quick and strong seam and gives a slightly raised finish to the edging. For a less raised seam, follow the same basic technique, but work each stitch in slip stitch rather than double crochet.

1 Start by lining up the two pieces with wrong sides together. Insert the hook in the top 2 loops of the stitch of the first piece, then into the corresponding stitch on the second piece.

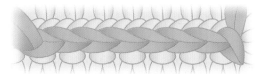

2 Complete the double crochet stitch as normal and continue on the next stitches as directed in the pattern. This gives a raised effect if the double crochet stitches are made on the right side of the work.

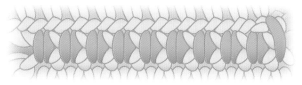

3 You can work with the wrong side of the work facing (with the pieces right side facing) if you don't want this effect and it still creates a good strong join.

Blocking

Crochet can tend to curl so to make flat pieces stay flat you may need to block them. Pin the piece out to the correct size and shape on the ironing board, then cover with a cloth and press or steam gently (depending on the type of yarn) and allow to dry completely. For some types of yarn it's best to soak or even just spritz with cold water, rather than using a steam iron.

Tassels and fringes

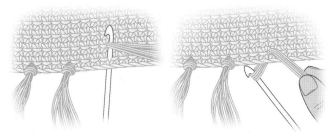

1 Cut yarn to quantity and length given in the pattern. Take suggested number of strands and fold in half. With right side of project facing, insert a crochet hook from the wrong side through one of the edge stitches. Catch the bunch of strands with the hook at the fold point.

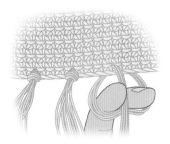

2 Pull through to make a big loop and, using your fingers, pull the tails of the bunch of strands through the loop.

3 Pull on the tails to tighten the loop firmly to secure the tassel.

CROCHET STITCH CONVERSION CHART

Crochet stitches are worked in the same way in both the UK and the USA, but the stitch names are not the same and identical names are used for different stitches. Below is a list of the UK terms used in this book, and the equivalent US terms.

UK TERM	US TERM
double crochet (dc)	single crochet (sc)
half treble (htr)	half double crochet (hdc)
treble (tr)	double crochet (dc)
double treble (dtr)	treble (tr)
triple treble (trtr)	double treble (dtr)
quadruple treble (qtr)	triple treble (trtr)
tension	gauge
yarn round hook (yrh)	yarn over hook (yoh)

SUPPLIERS

Choosing yarns is one of the most enjoyable aspects of starting a new crochet project! However, with so many colours, fibres and brands to choose from it can sometimes be hard to know just where to start. Here are a selection of the brands that have been featured in the projects in this book, so you can shop these brands, or team them with something from your stash!

Bernat
www.loveknitting.com
www.yarnspirations.com

Berroco
www.berroco.com
www.loveknitting.com

Brown Sheep Company
www.loveknitting.com
www.brownsheep.com

Cascade
www.cascadeyarns.com
www.loveknitting.com

Caron
www.loveknitting.com
www.yarnspirations.com

Lily Sugar 'n Cream
www.hobbycraft.co.uk
www.joann.com

Lion Brand
www.lionbrand.com
www.loveknitting.com

Paintbox
www.loveknitting.com

Rowan
www.knitrowan.com
www.loveknitting.com
www.jimmybeanswool.com

Schachenmayr
www.loveknitting.com

Stylecraft Yarns
www.stylecraft-yarns.co.uk
www.loveknitting.com

World of Wool
www.worldofwool.co.uk

For tools and finishings, the following have store locators on their websites, as well as online sales.

UK

John Lewis
www.johnlewis.co.uk

Hobbycraft
www.hobbycraft.co.uk

USA

Michaels
www.michaels.com

Jo-Ann Fabric and Craft Stores
www.joann.com

If you wish to substitute a different yarn for the one recommended in the pattern, try the Yarnsub website for suggestions:

Yarnsub
www.yarnsub.com

ACKNOWLEDGEMENTS

Huge thanks to Cindy Richards, Penny Craig and the team at CICO Books. Thank you also to Marie Clayton and Jemima Bicknell for ensuring the patterns are the best they could be and to the photographers, and stylists, for making everything so stunning!

I would also like to send my thanks to the fantastic yarn companies that continue to support my designs with yarns – Brown Sheep Yarns, Cascade Yarns, Love Knitting, Rowan – your generosity is hugely appreciated.

I adore crochet and loved having this opportunity to experiment with the different styles, techniques and colour combinations that make up the collection for this book. Thank you for the continued support and encouragement from my online friends and readers of www.madepeachy.com

To my sweet family, John, Wolfie and Waffle, thank you for supporting me every step of the way!

INDEX